"Rebecca St. James writes as beautifully as she sings, and about one of the most beautiful gifts we've been given . . . a chaste sexuality. Her witness and wisdom, winsomely given, is persuasive encouragement to live God's gift in God's way."

—EUGENE H. PETERSON
Translator of *The Message* Bible and Professor Emeritus of Spiritual Theology, Regent College, Vancouver, B.C.

"The first time I heard the song 'Wait for Me' my response was 'Wow!' I feel the same way about the book. It's romantic, real, and challenging. Packed with Scripture, it shows just how good following God's plan can be. This is a message that Rebecca lives. Her example and personal faithfulness make it powerful."

—JOSHUA HARRIS
Best-selling author of *I Kissed Dating Goodbye* and *Boy Meets Girl*

"Rebecca St. James's *Wait for Me* is a survival guide for all who are walking the perilous premarital minefields. She gives us a practical, frank, and loving handbook on how to avoid a lifetime of heartbreak and regret, yet she offers hope and healing for the casualties of 'love' and lust. Never have we needed this kind of candid encouragement more."

—JON RIVERS
20: The Countdown Magazine

"With warmth, compassion, and a depth of understanding and knowledge of God's Word, Rebecca St. James touches the core of the purity message in a way that young people will certainly relate to and appreciate. This young woman has lived what she writes, making a choice to honor God with her life in the midst of peer pressures and social messages that continually call to all of us—especially the young—to compromise. *Wait for Me* is a relevant and timely book, with a message that will touch a lot of lives with the good news that—with God's help—right choices are now and always ours for the making."

—Josh McDowell
Author/Speaker

"Rebecca's 'Wait for Me' song was hugely popular with our readers, and not just because it was a catchy tune. It's because Rebecca sensitively tackles a topic—sexual purity—vital to all Christian teens. This book takes that song's message and expounds on it—biblically, graciously—in friend-to-friend fashion. *Wait for Me* is a message of encouragement to those who are committed to abstinence until their wedding day. And it's a message of hope and forgiveness to those who have made mistakes. Good words indeed."

—Mark Moring
Campus Life magazine

Wait for Me

REDISCOVERING THE JOY OF PURITY IN ROMANCE

REBECCA ST. JAMES
WITH DALE REEVES

THOMAS NELSON
Since 1798

NASHVILLE   DALLAS   MEXICO CITY   RIO DE JANEIRO   BEIJING

Published in Nashville, Tennessee, by Thomas Nelson. Thomas Nelson is a registered trademark of Thomas Nelson, Inc.

Published in association with the literary agency of Alive Communications, 7680 Goddard Street, Suite 200, Colorado Springs, CO 80920 (www.alivecommunications.com).

Thomas Nelson, Inc., titles may be purchased in bulk for educational, business, fund-raising, or sales promotional use. For information, please e-mail SpecialMarkets@ThomasNelson.com.

Scripture quotations noted NIV are from the HOLY BIBLE: NEW INTERNATIONAL VERSION®. © 1973, 1978, 1984 by International Bible Society. Used by permission of Zondervan Publishing House. All rights reserved.

Scripture quotations noted THE MESSAGE are from *The Message: The New Testament in Contemporary English.* © 1993 by Eugene H. Peterson. Used by permission of NavPress Publishing Group.

Scripture quotations noted NLT are from the *Holy Bible*, New Living Translation, © 1996. Used by permission of Tyndale House Publishers, Inc., Wheaton, Illinois 60189. All rights reserved.

Scripture quotations noted NCV are from the New Century Version®. © 2005 by Thomas Nelson, Inc. Used by permission. All rights reserved.

Page Design by Casey Hooper

Library of Congress Cataloging-in-Publication Data

St. James, Rebecca.
  Wait for me : rediscovering the joy of purity in romance / Rebecca St. James with Dale Reeves.
    p. cm.
  ISBN 978-0-7852-7127-7 (hc)
  ISBN 978-0-7852-8825-1 (tp)
  ISBN 978-1-4003-1287-0 (rpk)
  1. Chastity. 2. Youth—Religious life. 3. Marriage--Religious aspects—Christianity. 4. Sexual abstinence--Religious aspects—Christianity. I. Reeves, Dale. II. Title.
  BV4647.C5 S7 2002
  241'.66—dc21
                                                                        2002006422

Printed in the United States of America

09 10 11 RRD 6 5 4 3 2

*To those whose regretful tears
inspired these pages.*

*Above all, to God;
may He use these words to bring hope
that will dry those tears,
and conviction to all—to keep
the tears from falling in the first place.*

CONTENTS

ACKNOWLEDGMENTS   ix

INTRODUCTION   xi

CHAPTER 1:   **DREAM AGAIN**   5
             Recovering the Dream of True Romance

CHAPTER 2:   **MIND MATTERS**   19
             Guarding Your Thoughts
             to Make Wise Decisions

CHAPTER 3:   **THE ECSTASY (OR AGONY) OF SEX**   39
             Why Waiting Is Best

CHAPTER 4:   **PROTECTING PURITY**   65
             Practical Ways to Wait in a Culture
             That Screams, "Just Do It!"

CONTENTS

CHAPTER 5:   LOVE AND MARRIAGE   89
              What It Is We're Waiting For

CHAPTER 6:   A SECOND CHANCE   113
              Forgiveness and Hope for
              the Guilt-Ridden and Hurting

CHAPTER 7:   I'M GLAD YOU ASKED!   133
              Q & A on Sexual Purity

STUDY GUIDE   147

ABOUT THE AUTHOR   185
NOTES   187

ACKNOWLEDGMENTS

I want to say thank you . . .

To God, my love, my inspiration, my protection, my life . . . I could go on forever! Anything good that comes from this book is You.

To Dale Reeves, my friend, advisor, Bible encyclopedia, and coworker with Christ. This book would not be without you. Thanks for all that you have sewn into this piece.

To Eric Welch, for believing from the start in a crazy idea! Thanks for being my friend and for making the beautiful, creative, and symbolic pictures that filled the first edition of this book. Perfect.

To Brian Hampton, for "going with it" and being such a team player. You're a joy to work with.

To Mum, Dad, Nanna, Pop, Karleen, and all of my friends whose stories I have shared in this book. The vulnerability, heart, experience, and wisdom you have given are priceless. I thank you from the bottom of my heart.

To the wonderful team at Thomas Nelson—Brian Hampton,

Kyle Olund, Belinda Bass, Kate Etue, and Blythe McIntosh—and Greg Johnson at Alive for dreaming with me and activating the dream.

To Teryn Turner and Josh Penner, for being the "perfect couple" for the first version of this book and to Najee for making them look extra beautiful (and handsome)!

To Ken Farley, for believing in the song "Wait for Me" and allowing it to be heard.

To Ben Smallbone, for your gracious help on this project.

To all at ForeFront and Smallbone Management, who have supported this song and broadened the reach of its message of purity.

To my great-grandma Beasley (1901–2002), who for 101 years lived as an example of godliness and purity.

To you, the reader of this book, for opening your heart enough to hear the ideas held in these pages. Rest in His perfect plan for you.

INTRODUCTION

It was summer and I was finishing up work on a new album called *Transform*. Finally it seemed we had all the songs we needed and the album was close to completion. Between working with four different producers and many months of writing and recording already under my belt, I was ready for this baby to be born! Close to the end of our production time, I headed to a place known as "The Gorge" in Washington State to sing at a large Christian festival called Creation.

There, backstage, I ran into a friend of mine, Josh Harris, author of *I Kissed Dating Goodbye*. Outside the food tent on that day, I had a conversation that would greatly influence my life and ministry. Josh, having been a friend for many years, knew and shared my passion for purity. Over and over he had heard me talk from the stage about the fact that true love does wait and that God's beautiful and best way is to save sex for marriage. For years I'd been talking about *one day* writing a purity song. So in the course of our conversation he asked me if I had written it yet and was it by any chance on this next album? I quickly let him know that I felt we had all the songs we needed for this project and that God was yet to give me inspiration for one about purity! Josh responded by telling me that he would ask God to bring this much needed song so that it could potentially be added to the project I was finishing. The story could have ended there, but as you know, God answered my friend's prayer. As I recall, it was only a couple days later, in my bunk on the tour bus, that the song "landed" in my head, and in about half an hour, lyrics were written and melodies formed. I truly see it as a miracle song.

Now, after all these years, it's hard for me to imagine life without "Wait for Me." In my life, it's been more than just another song—it became a calling and a catalyst for the book you hold in your hands.

It's been a joy to see this work also translated into multiple languages and to know that it has helped young people know how to live in purity. One thing I know, God is raising up a pure generation around the world, and the fact that you are reading this right now hints that you have or are considering joining us! I pray that this is so!

So there's the abbreviated biography of the life of this book so far.

I'm forever grateful to Josh for being an inspirational friend who was used by God. Thank you, Dale, for being such a great partner in this project. Thanks Thomas Nelson for reprinting it all these times! And above all, thank you Jesus for this better idea, this pure, beautiful way of love that brings abundant life . . . All glory to You!

A WORD ABOUT JOURNAL PAGES

A few years ago, I started writing love letters to my future husband. These letters have been an inspiration to me, and I have found that it really helps brighten the waiting process to write these love letters in expectation of one day giving them to my future husband. I also feel that it is something my future mate will really enjoy . . . catching glimpses into my life and thoughts at different stages of my journey.

Throughout this book you will find starter ideas and space where you will be able to express your heart, thoughts, and ideas—written words that will one day be a treasure to your future mate. As you live in sexual purity, enjoy dreaming and sharing those dreams with the one you are waiting for. Enjoy constructing with words a "time capsule" of memories for your future mate to one day discover.

Together living for Jesus,
Rebecca St. James
Eph. 3:20

WAIT FOR ME

By Rebecca St. James

Darling, did you know that I
I dream about you
Waiting for the look in your eyes
When we meet for the first time
Darling, did you know that I
I pray about you
Praying that you will hold on
Keep your loving eyes only for me
I am waiting for
Praying for you, darling
Wait for me too
Wait for me as I wait for you
I am waiting for
Praying for you, darling
Wait for me too
Wait for me, as I wait for you
Darling, wait
Darling did you know I dream
about life together
Knowing it will be forever
I'll be yours and you'll be mine

And darling when I say
'Til death do us part
I'll mean it with all of my heart
Now and always, faithful to you

I am waiting for
Praying for you, darling
Wait for me too
Wait for me as I wait for you
I am waiting for
Praying for you, darling
Wait for me too
Wait for me, as I wait for you
Darling, wait

Now I know you may have made mistakes
But there's forgiveness and
a second chance
So wait for me darling
Wait for me
Wait for me

I am waiting for
Praying for you, darling
Wait for me too
Wait for me as I wait for you

I am waiting for
Praying for you, darling
Wait for me too
Wait for me, as I wait for you
Darling, wait

© 2000 Up in the Mix Music (BMI)/Bibbitsong Music (Admin. by ICG)

You've dreamed the dream many times...

You're lost and alone in darkened woods with danger lurking around every corner. You're cold, hungry, and tired. *Where did I lose my way?* you wonder. You try to turn back, but every tree looks the same and each step only makes you feel more alone.

Then suddenly you hear the sound of a large beast thundering in your direction, making the ground tremble beneath you. In a panic you look for a place to hide.

At last the creature bursts into the clearing, stopping inches away from where you are seated, completely terrified, on the ground. To your great surprise, instead of a terrifying animal, you glimpse a powerful stallion carrying a tall, dark, and handsome rider. The man smiles at you, a smile that reaches his eyes, and you know immediately that you can trust him.

All fear vanishes as he dismounts his horse to accompany you out of the forest and safely to your home. Before you know it, you

1

are scooped up into his arms, placed gently on the horse, and expertly taken from the terror of the forest, out into open spaces and the sun's warm rays.

As you ride off into the sunset, you feel like flying and know that not only will life never be the same, but this might just be the "happily ever after" of which you have always dreamed.

The call has gone out from the king to find and rescue his only daughter, the princess. She has been abducted by the corrupt Dark Lord, and the king has promised her hand in marriage to whoever can return her safely to her own kingdom.

You are aware of the extreme danger of the mission: you must successfully navigate alligator-infested waters; trek through forests filled with wild creatures, quicksand, and quagmire; and climb a steep seaside cliff that leads to the Dark Lord's fortress. Many a knight has lost his life in pursuit of the beautiful damsel who dreams of true love's rescue from the clutches of evil. But you have the fortitude to overcome every obstacle. You are a champion warrior, and your steed is up to the challenge.

You nimbly traverse your way through the swamp and forest, defeating countless bloodthirsty creatures as you go. You then skillfully ascend the treacherous juts of the seaside precipice.

But just as you step foot on the Dark Lord's territory, you are greeted by his two henchmen. You draw your double-edged sword

from its scabbard, and your enemies soon wish they had not picked this fight. With relentless courage you attack and parry, felling the Dark Lord's evil minions.

As you leave the wounded warriors on the ground behind you, you are met with another dangerous challenge: the guardian of the moat—a great, fire-breathing dragon. With all the bravery and strength within you, and the faithful sword by your side, you triumph over the beast, against all odds. The arm wound inflicted by the dragon is but a small price to pay for the joy that awaits in the tower.

All obstacles removed, you scale the fortress with the agility of a rock climber, crashing through the tower's window to rescue the princess. As you sweep her into your arms, she gazes at you with radiant eyes of adoration, knowing you are the true love she has dreamed of. Your heart feels the same.

Swiftly you escape through the tower window and flee on foot toward the shore. As you rappel down the cliff to your awaiting steed, your own dreams begin. You envision everlasting love with your bride-to-be . . .

CHAPTER *one*

Dream Again

RECOVERING THE DREAM OF TRUE ROMANCE

> Darling, did you know that I dream about you
> Waiting for the look in your eyes
> When we meet for the first time[1]

THE DREAM

If you're a girl, perhaps you've grown up with the desire to be rescued by a knight in shining armor. If you're a guy, maybe you've thought about being the knight who rescues his princess. In either case, is it only a dream or is it a God-given desire, purposely placed within you by God Himself?

I believe that God has placed "The Dream" inside each one of

5

us, unless He has specifically called you to singleness. We each have a desire for intimacy, for someone to know us fully and love us completely. We long to be able to share our hearts and still find acceptance. A guy longs to protect; a girl longs to be protected. And that's exactly the way God created us. When we follow His plan, there are great blessings in store.

> "For I know the plans I have for you," declares the LORD, "plans to prosper you and not to harm you, plans to give you hope and a future. Then you will call upon me and come and pray to me, and I will listen to you. You will seek me and find me when you seek me with all your heart."
>
> (JER. 29:11–13 NIV)

Unfortunately, in this culture today, so many people have given up on "The Dream," and have chosen to accept something less than God intended for them. As one girl said to me, "I was about ready to give up any kind of hope that there are any guys out there who are willing to wait (sexually and emotionally) for the one that God will bring to them in His perfect time . . . I've always known a few girls who want to wait, but I actually read e-mails from (gasp!) guys who were saying the same thing. That is so rare to find. God's way is truly best!"

I hope that in these pages I have helped to defy a modern misconception: that romance can be fun and exciting only when it involves breaking the rules. Immorality is glamorized everywhere: on TV, in movies, and in most music today. What the entertainers don't show or sing about is the very unglamorous, often agonizing consequences of an immoral lifestyle. Truth is, the most joyful, beautiful, exciting romance is the one that is pure. It is also the most free! Pure romance is not bound by sexual addiction or selfish motives and desires. It is free to love within God's perfect boundaries.

> "It is for freedom that Christ has set us free. Stand firm, then, and do not let yourselves be burdened again by a yoke of slavery. . . . You, my brothers, were called to be free. But do not use your freedom to indulge the sinful nature; rather, serve one another in love."
>
> (GAL. 5:1, 13 NIV)

FULFILLED DREAMS

Can you picture with me the joy of the couple that has waited? They have a wonderful storybook wedding with family and friends wishing them well. The bride wears white, truly signifying the purity of her heart and body.

As a special part of the wedding ceremony, the groom gives his bride a ring that he has worn on a chain around his neck, a symbol of his own commitment to sexual purity. It has helped him remain strong in his promise to God and to her for the years leading up to this beautiful day. She receives the ring with tears in her eyes.

Hours later the groom carries his bride over the threshold of the cabin that is to be the honeymoon suite. He soon has a cheery fire burning in the fireplace, and after unpacking a few things, his joyful bride approaches him with an expectant, trusting, and contented smile on her face. As he reaches out to enfold her in his arms, both know that they are united with God's blessing and protection on their mutual commitment of love within marriage. They are now ready to learn and make many first-time memories together.

I received a letter from an eighteen-year-old guy who expressed these thoughts:

> At the moment I am trying to buy a "wait for me" ring; I want it so badly because I got this amazing picture in my head one night in church, and I am going to try my hardest to make it come true. I was picturing my wedding day. Imagine how great it would be if I wore the ring from now until that day. My wife and I look at each other, dedicate our lives to each other, exchange vows, and then we exchange rings. When she looks down at my hand, I want her to see the ring, the ring that states that I've waited my whole life just for her, and then she takes that ring off

and replaces it with a new one, one that shows that I no longer have to wait ... that she is here. I think that will be one of the most beautiful pictures in my entire life. This is the God-intended dream that can actually come true.

"Blessed are the pure in heart, for they will see God."
(MATT. 5:8 NIV)

IN GOD'S HANDS

Several years ago I was asked to play the part of Mary in a touring Christmas musical called "Child of the Promise." I thoroughly enjoyed learning the songs I was to sing, as well as the other characters' songs. One that was especially meaningful to me was Elizabeth's song, appropriately named "When the Dream Never Dies."

In the book of Luke, we learn that Elizabeth was Mary's relative. Elizabeth had a dream: for years she had desired to have a baby. But as time passed and Elizabeth had already reached old age, everyone believed she would never have her longed-for child. Then an angel appeared to her husband, Zechariah, foretelling that she would bear a son named John.

Today I prayed for you that . . .

_____

_____

_____

_____

_____

_____

_____

_____

_____

_____

_____

_____

_____

_____

_____

_____

_____

_____

_____

_____

_____

In the musical, when Elizabeth discovered she was pregnant, this is the song she sang out of gratitude to God:

Deep in my heart was an ember of longing
Kept warm by the flame of desire
A dream held in secret I yearned to hold openly
Fanned by my hope into fire
It burned to such heat I could touch it no more
So I put it away and then closed up the door
Forever extinguishing all that would keep it alive
But the dream never died
The Lord has done this for me, he has looked on me kindly
He has heard all my cries
He has given me back what I laid at his feet
It must be God, when the dream never dies
Isn't it just like the Lord to invite me
To put all my dreams in his hands
Forever releasing the grip that once held them
Forever surrendering my plans?
And then when he's certain it's not born of men
He calls for the fire to rekindle again
And he asks me to know in my heart what's not seen with my eyes
So the dream never dies.[2]

I not only love the hope that is in this song but also the challenge to "put all my dreams in his hands" and "forever surrender my plans." For we can know and trust the fact that, as the old TV show said, "Father knows best."

"Love is patient."
(1 Cor. 13:4 niv)

RESET BUTTON

The reason so many of us have lost sight of the dream is because our culture has trained us to think a certain way; it has sold us the lie that the dream is not possible. I was saying to a friend just the other day that I believe a lot of people get married today largely out of fear that they will be left behind and left alone. They don't wait for their soul mates, or the best friends with whom they want to spend the rest of their lives, because they've lost sight of the dream . . . or maybe they never believed in it in the first place.

When the dream has been lost, misplaced, or just covered up by disappointment, we need to dream again, to reset our thinking.

I have a beloved old hair dryer that I inherited from a house guest who accidentally left it behind. This hair dryer does its job very nicely, not too "blowy," not too hot—just right. But for this lovely "Old Red" hair dryer to work its magic, the reset button has to be pressed every time. Otherwise it just sits there, incapable of action.

I think that old hair dryer is a little like us. Unless we press

My hopes for our future together are . . .

_____

_____

_____

_____

_____

_____

_____

_____

_____

_____

_____

_____

_____

_____

_____

_____

_____

_____

_____

_____

that button to reset our thinking, we are paralyzed by our fear, by our past, or by thoughts from our culture. By staying paralyzed and not experiencing the freedom of complete trust in Jesus, I believe we often keep the dream from being realized. Let go, my friend. Recover the dream.

Even though there are guys who seem to be looking for "easy" girls, I really believe that their hearts' desire is to find someone who has never given herself to anyone, and will only do so when she has found her lifelong companion. That's because God placed that desire in their hearts. This is the ideal, the dream, but for many the dream has been lost, shattered, or torn into a thousand pieces. Now you may be willing to settle for so much less than what God intended.

For some of you this book will be like preventive medicine, a shot that will hopefully keep you from making big mistakes. For others of you, your dream has been stolen from you, or willingly given but then regretted. May this be a book of healing and protection from this day on! To those of you who have already given in to sexual temptation, the next two chapters may seem to point a finger. But please read them carefully and know that my desire is to encourage you as well as to inspire those who haven't stumbled. I hope that after you read them you will be aware of your choices from here on—no matter what is in your past. This is a book of beauty, of joy, of forgiveness . . . of hope.

"Create in me a pure heart, O God, and renew a steadfast spirit within me."

(Ps. 51:10 NIV)

Lord Jesus, thank You for placing "The Dream" in my heart. Lord, I know You have promised that You have plans to prosper me and not harm me, to give me hope and a future. Help me to be strong in the knowledge that You have a perfect plan for my life. I want to trust You. I lay my future at Your feet. I put my life in Your hands. I bring any shattered dreams to You for healing. Here and now I ask You to reset my thinking. Help me to dream again.

I love You, Lord,

In Your name, Amen.

When I imagine our life together . . .

_____

_____

_____

_____

_____

_____

_____

_____

_____

_____

_____

_____

_____

_____

_____

_____

_____

_____

Mind Matters

A fifteen-year-old girl e-mailed me with her story:

> About a year ago I got into some pretty tough stuff. I gave in to my own sexual desires and trapped myself in porn. I let it control me. I was a practicing Christian before I was trapped. So when I would surround myself with this, God kept giving me signals and warnings to stop and turn back, or else things would get really nasty in my life. I didn't listen. I didn't really want to hear from God at that time.
>
> Close to the summer I confessed to my boyfriend what I was doing with my free time. He, surprisingly, understood but could not offer me any help.
>
> That summer I went on a mission trip to Mexico. I spent all ten of those days refocusing myself on God, and I asked him to come back into my life. A few weeks

later, on a youth retreat, I confessed my sins to my closest friends. . . .

At one of your concerts, God spoke through you. I gave up absolutely everything to God, and more importantly, I asked him for help. It worked. God helped me. He forgave me of my wrongdoings and remains patient with me when I slip up every now and then. There's a long road still to travel, but I know in my heart that God's there to help all the way.

CHAPTER two

Mind Matters

GUARDING YOUR THOUGHTS TO MAKE WISE DECISIONS

> Darling, did you know that I pray about you
> Praying that you will hold on
> Keep your loving eyes only for me

THE EYES DON'T LIE

Have you ever really looked into the eyes of a small, happy child? There is such light and joy there. Often, though, if a child grows to an age of accountability and does not give his or her heart to Jesus, that light of innocence and purity is lost. There are a few adults in my life in whom I especially see that beautiful, childlike joy. My worship leader, my grandma, a singer/friend of mine—all of them exhibit a special light that radiates. It's a purity of conscience, a childlike wonder at life and the simple love of Jesus that shines forth through their eyes. I desire that in my own life and in my eyes.

On the other hand, I have also known people in my life who, either because of shame, pain that has not been dealt with, or many other possible reasons, can barely look me in the eye.

"The eye is the lamp of the body. If your eyes are good, your whole body will be full of light. But if your eyes are bad, your whole body will be full of darkness. If then the light within you is darkness, how great is that darkness!"

(Matt. 6:22–23 niv)

If the eye is the "lamp of the body," then we should be very careful what we allow to gain entry into our minds through our eyes. Our eyes have also been referred to as "the windows of the soul," so we really need to put spiritual blinders on to protect our hearts and minds. Perhaps your eyes have allowed images into your mind that were ungodly and impure. Yet no matter what the past may have been, there is still a way to purity of the eyes, where light replaces the darkness. It is a matter of surrendering the past, present, and future completely to Jesus. Even when we think no one is watching, we must be faithful to live for Him, in

His way and His light. Since our eyes say so much about our lives and how we have lived them (or are *living* them), the lack of light, taken away by deeds of darkness, *will* show—in our lives, in our eyes, or in eternity's unveiling.

> "Have nothing to do with the fruitless deeds of darkness, but rather expose them. For it is shameful even to mention what the disobedient do in secret. But everything exposed by the light becomes visible."
> (Eph. 5:11–13 NIV)

After Adam and Eve sinned in the Garden of Eden, they ran and hid from God in an attempt to cover their shame. Guilt is a very powerful thing. It clouds one's vision and can really paralyze a person. That's exactly what Satan wants. After he tempts us to sin (as he did Adam and Eve), then he continually throws that sin back in our faces, whispering, "You're not really worthy of God's affection, so you might as well give up." He is all about temptation, and then accusation. He wants nothing less than to condemn you, make you carry around a lot of guilt, and ultimately destroy you.

One of Satan's greatest tools is isolation. He loves to tempt you when you are alone, whispering, "No one will ever have to find out." And to combat him, we need to seek out some trusted friends who can help keep us accountable in this area.

Things I hope we have in common are . . . .

THE POWER OF THE MIND

God created the human brain as a computer with an unbelievable memory capacity. Your brain is able to recall thoughts and images from many years ago. It has been well documented that when one views pornography, powerful biochemical reactions kick in that can lead to addiction. When someone is excited by an image, the adrenal gland in his or her body secretes a chemical called epinephrine into the bloodstream, and the visual image eventually lodges itself in the brain. That explains why many adults say they can still recall the first pornographic image they ever viewed. God wants to spare you the pain of such an addiction. So the simple message is this: don't even begin to play with the fire, or you'll get burned.

> "You know the next commandment pretty well, too: 'Don't go to bed with another's spouse.' But don't think you've preserved your virtue simply by staying out of bed. Your heart can be corrupted by lust even quicker than your body. Those leering looks you think nobody notices—they also corrupt.
>
> "Let's not pretend this is easier than it really is. If you want to live a morally pure life, here's what you have to do: You have to blind your right eye the moment you catch it in a lustful leer. You have to choose to live one-eyed or else be dumped on a moral trash pile. And you have to chop off your

right hand the moment you notice it raised threateningly. Better a bloody stump than your entire being discarded for good in the dump."

(MATT. 5:27–30 THE MESSAGE, EMPHASIS MINE)

"Turn my eyes away from worthless things; preserve my life according to your word."

(PS. 119:37 NIV)

ALL ELSE FADES

On days off, from time to time, I visit a bed-and-breakfast. It is a wonderful time to be still, play, rest, read, sometimes fast, and just be . . . with God. I have had some amazingly memorable times when I'm there. One trip in particular stands out in my mind. I was sitting on the front porch of the house, watching the sunset. It was that time of the day when you can face the sun without being blinded by its usual brightness. I had been gazing quite intently at the sky in the direction of the sun when a bird caught my attention in a nearby tree. I shifted my eyes to look at it, and all of a sudden, my vision blacked out for a moment. I had to blink my eyes a few times to restore vision enough to see the bird. I realized that my eyes had so adjusted to the brightness of the western sky that the things around me had faded into the background and could not be seen as long as my eyes stayed focused toward the sun. I felt God speak to my spirit with a spiritual parallel to this picture. When we focus our eyes on the Son, Jesus, then the things of this world, its temptations, worries, fears, and hurts pale in significance. They fade into the background. I am reminded of a familiar song:

Turn your eyes upon Jesus,
look full in his wonderful face,
and the things of earth will grow strangely dim
in the light of his glory and grace.

If we are focused on Him, everything in the background will vanish away. That's what it means to have purity of heart, being single-minded, focused on what will please the One who created us.

> "So if you're serious about living this new resurrection life with Christ, act like it. Pursue the things over which Christ presides. Don't shuffle along, eyes to the ground, absorbed with the things right in front of you. Look up, and be alert to what is going on around Christ—that's where the action is. See things from his perspective."
>
> (Col. 3:1–2 The Message)

> "You will keep in perfect peace him whose mind is steadfast, because he trusts in you."
>
> (Isa. 26:3 niv)

AVOIDING TEMPTATION

Not too long ago I had the opportunity to sing at Billy Graham's ministry headquarters in Minneapolis, Minnesota. It was great because I was able to share with the staff how much I admire Mr. Graham. He is a hero of the faith to me. His consistency, his love for Jesus, and mostly his integrity speak volumes into my life. I have heard many stories of how he conducts himself that have impressed me greatly. I have heard people say that he has televisions removed from his hotel rooms so he won't be tempted to watch shows he knows he shouldn't. He will not ride in a car with another woman unless his wife is present.

This impressed me so much that I desired to take a similar stand, to the point of personal embarrassment. I have remained strong on this. One time I sent a male runner back to the concert hall to pick up a female so that we could drive the short distance from the hotel to the concert venue together. I want to avoid even the appearance of evil. Apart from my own protection from very unlikely, compromising events, someone could see me getting out of the car, alone with a man, and think, *I wonder what they've been up to?*

It's the same for you; when you are a college student you may think that it's OK to have a guy come into your dorm room during the day when you're alone. But what about the person down the hall who knows you're a Christian and sees you walk out of the room together? Through our actions we preach to those who don't know God. What are your actions saying to unbelievers?

Most of the time we don't even think about things like that. We think, *I have a hard enough time making the right decisions in the big issues of life, let alone those little areas.*

C'mon, Rebecca, you're thinking. But you know what? It's compromise in those little areas that lead to majorly bad decisions later. It's strength and courage shown in the "small" tests of life that make the "big" decisions easy.

> "How can a young person live a clean life? By carefully reading the map of your Word. I'm single-minded in pursuit of you; don't let me miss the road signs you've posted."
> (Ps. 119:9–10 The Message)

> "But among you there must not be even a hint of sexual immorality, or of any kind of impurity, or of greed, because these are improper for God's holy people."
> (Eph. 5:3 niv)

> "Avoid every kind of evil."
> (1 Thess. 5:22 niv)

YOUR SANCTUARY

As we pray for our future spouses, we're going to be challenged to keep our eyes only for them as well. Do you remember this song?

Lord, prepare me, to be a sanctuary,
Pure and holy, tried and true.
With thanksgiving I'll be a living
Sanctuary for you[1]

This song preaches a very good message in a short amount of words. When we give our lives to God, we become His sanctuary or "holy place," pure and set apart for Him. The song also strongly states that being tried and tested is a part of being a sanctuary for God. We will be tested in our purity. But this is where we are given the chance to be *true*. I love the last phrase, "With thanksgiving I'll be a living sanctuary for you." It is a joyful, wonderful thing to live a pure, conscience-clear life before God. It is something for which we can be incredibly grateful to God!

"Or don't you know that your body is the temple of the Holy Spirit, who lives in you and was given to you by God?"
(1 COR. 6:19 NLT)

PERCEPTION PROTECTION

When we choose to look at things that are damaging to us (pictures, videos, movies, CD covers), it distorts our perception of reality. Guys, if you choose to look at pornography, realize that what you are doing sets you up for problems later. No woman

I hope you are . . .

can live up to the impossible standards depicted in those magazines, videos, or Web sites. Because of computer technology, you're not really looking at reality anyway. Pornography also encourages a demeaning attitude toward women by depicting them as playthings, objects to be used and discarded. This will affect the way you treat girls now, and even your wife in the future. God's Word admonishes you to treat them with respect and absolute purity, as "sisters" in the family of God. And girls, as we saw from the opening story in this chapter, the visual temptations aren't just a "guy thing." God is very concerned with what we put in our minds as well. Whether it's porn or "soft porn," we all need to be on our guards, asking God for the strength to overcome our fleshly desires.

> "Do not rebuke an older man harshly, but exhort him as if he were your father. Treat younger men as brothers, older women as mothers, and younger women as sisters, with absolute purity."
>
> (1 TIM. 5:1–2 NIV)

My nanna (grandma) has passed on some great advice that has helped in my pursuit of purity of mind, heart, and body. Here is some of her practical wisdom: "In the area of purity, television doesn't help. At one stage double beds weren't even allowed to be shown on TV, and now you see people making love! As soon as I see an R-rated movie coming on, I turn it off. Don't watch movies that display immoral activity because *we learn through seeing*. You might say you can 'handle it,' but Satan is sneaky, and he creeps in, conditioning our minds to accept wrong things. Before we know it, these things become actions in our lives."

WHAT ARE YOU WEARING?

A guy wrote to thank me for my emphasis on modesty. He described one of his pet peeves: "Women don't want to be treated poorly or like an object, yet many women continue to dress inappropriately." Can I just say something to the girls? I think it is so important that we dress so as not to cause our brothers to stumble. Onstage and offstage I am very careful about what I wear for two reasons: First, I don't want to lead guys astray who are watching. And second, I don't want to hurt my sisters in the audience who might be influenced by what I wear. I make sure I'm not showing too much skin (especially too much of my back, arms, and chest), and I watch to make sure that my clothes aren't too tight.

I'll admit, girls, it can really be a challenge to find clothes that are hip, modern, funky . . . and modest. But it is worth the effort. This doesn't just apply to me because I'm on stage—this applies to you too! William Shakespeare wrote the famous line, "All the world's a stage, and all the men and women merely players." That's true, and people are watching you. I don't want to get to heaven and have God let me know that I was so busy trying to look "cool" that I was hurting His sons! I'm sure you don't want that either!

One last thing. I will always remember the time our missions director's wife came and spoke to our youth group about modesty. She was really practical in the things she shared, and one thing in particular stood out to me. She said that to figure out how long skirts or shorts should be (at least), let your arm hang naturally against your body. A good indication of where your clothing should cover is where your fingertips reach on your leg. I think that's a good rule to go by. You might think this rule is a bit prudish by today's standards, but God expects His people to live by different principles than those espoused by the world. He wants us to rise above what everybody else is doing. You may choose to follow a different guideline than the one explained above, but the point is to carefully think through your standards of dress.

Kelly Patterson, the lady who spoke, found it hard to talk about this subject, but the reason she did was because a few of the guys in the youth group had complained about how some of the girls in the group dressed. Apparently the guys just didn't know where to look—there was too much skin. Girls, let's do our brothers a favor—let's exemplify purity in our hearts, actions . . . and in the way we dress.

> "I made a solemn pact with myself never to undress a girl
> with my eyes."
>
> (Job 31:1 The Message)

"I'm doing the very best I can, and I'm doing it at home, where it counts. I refuse to take a second look at corrupting people and degrading things."

(Ps. 101:2–3 The Message)

GOOD FOOD FOR THOUGHT

In this chapter I've focused a lot on what to avoid, how to keep your eyes away from evil. But there are *many* things that you can watch, read, listen to, look at, and download that are healthy for a solid Christian life. Several good Christian Web sites are available that are wonderful resources for filling your mind with good things. Christian books and magazines are also great (I have a weakness for Christian historical fiction). Today, there is a lot of music that promotes Christian values, TV (some, anyway) that aids learning, and from time to time you can also find a good wholesome movie or two. I personally love romantic comedies like *The Wedding Planner*, *While You Were Sleeping*, and *Emma*, which are fun and not "morally damaging." A couple of good sources for evaluating movies and TV shows from a Christian perspective are:

http://www.ministryandmedia.com/
http://www.cinemainfocus.com/
http://www.nappaland.com/

When I picture you, I picture . . .

Above all, the best rule of thumb for testing whether or not something is good or bad for your mind is Philippians 4:8: "Summing it all up, friends, I'd say you'll do best by filling your minds and meditating on things true, noble, reputable, authentic, compelling, gracious—the best, not the worst; the beautiful, not the ugly; things to praise, not things to curse" (THE MESSAGE).

The Ecstasy (or Agony) of Sex

A guy in his twenties from Michigan recently shared this story with me:

> My teenage and college years have been full of temptation, but I am still holding out for my wife. . . . When I was eleven years old, my older sister got pregnant, then a few years later, my older brother got himself into trouble too. He was caught with a girl in my parents' bed, then was promptly thrown out of the house for his actions. . . . Many of my friends claimed to have had sex, but it was the quiet, broken ones that always drew my attention. They would be sitting off to one side, and you could tell they were hurting. When asked, they would say nothing. When I did get some information from them, it was often the same thing— they were with individuals whom they believed loved

them, had sex with them, and then their companions left them. They had placed their hearts, bodies, and souls on the line for these people, only to have them thrown back into their faces. The despondent looks on the faces of those friends were heartbreaking, further driving home the message that I had to wait, if not for the sake of my future wife, then for the sake of each soul that came in contact with me.

By waiting, you do not have any regrets about what happened, because nothing has happened. You will never have to be in the position of having to list all your past sexual partners, because you have none. You will never be dissatisfied that your spouse is not as experienced as a previous partner, because there will be none to compare. . . . We are commanded to love one another as Christ loved us. Premarital sex is not just about you and the person you are with. It is about you, your future spouse, the person you are with, and his or her future spouse. What you do in one night will change the lives of at least four people. It is better to wait and be in God's will than to follow your own sinful desires and be miserable afterward.

CHAPTER three

The Ecstasy (or Agony) of Sex

WHY WAITING IS BEST

> I am waiting for, praying for you, darling
> Wait for me too
> Wait for me as I wait for you

SHATTERED DREAMS

Imagine with me for a minute this scenario:

A girl and a guy choose to sleep together for the first time. He desires her physically, and though warning signs are going off in his head, he ignores them and continues on to where he has not let himself go before. He enjoys the physical rush, but afterward tries to shoo away the feelings of guilt, the conviction that all he has done is use her.

She is needy and enjoys the sensations his touch evokes, but at the same time feels scared and used. Both take showers afterward and try to wash away the feelings of uncleanness. There was no lasting love that was felt before or after, just lust. A week later the couple breaks up and the agony of having given themselves completely begins. They have become one flesh, but without true love or commitment.

Since I don't understand the agony that comes from having sex outside of marriage, I wanted you to hear from someone who does. A girl I've only met through the mail described her experience:

> My parents had always told me to wait until I was married. Although I had kept this desire alive in my heart, I somehow got lost along the way. When I was seventeen years old, I started dating a non-Christian, and I thought I had really found true love. After some time, though, I guess he was bored with me, so he decided to break up with me. I was so afraid of losing him that I told him I was ready to give myself to him. He was shocked, and tried to talk me out of it (he had known how important waiting was for me), but I just

told him I didn't care anymore. I told him I really loved him and that I was sorry he hadn't felt satisfied with me.

So in my bedroom I had sex with him. I just kept telling myself over and over again that I wasn't really doing what I was about to do. My entire body went numb—I didn't feel a thing! I closed my eyes tightly and waited for what seemed like hours. I tried to act normal and happy, and tried to pretend that I had enjoyed the experience as well. I felt sick, and I just wanted him to go away. After he left, I just stayed under the covers and thought that I could never pray to God again because I had just turned my back on Him. The next day I called up my boyfriend and told him I didn't want to see him again.

The dream had been shattered. She went on in her letter to tell me that it took her quite a long time to forgive herself and to accept God's forgiveness; then she closed with this statement, "Making love is something so worthwhile to wait for, and I know it can only be beautiful inside of marriage."

"Run from anything that stimulates youthful lust. Follow anything that makes you want to do right. Pursue faith and

love and peace, and enjoy the companionship of those who
call on the LORD with pure hearts."

(2 TIM. 2:22 NLT)

WHAT WOULD GOD THINK?

How many times have you and I heard the age-old question, how
far is too far? I don't even have to tell you that I'm talking about
sexual intimacy; you've heard the question enough to know. You
may have even asked it yourself. I believe the answer is extremely
simple and its core idea comes directly from the Bible: "Whatever
you do, do it all for the glory of God" (1 Cor. 10:31 NIV); "Whatever you do . . . do it *all* in the name of the Lord Jesus (Col. 3:17
NIV, emphasis mine).

If you are a follower of Jesus, then the first question you need
to ask yourself when relating to the opposite sex (in both emotional and physical matters) is, what would God think? That is
really the bottom-line question, not only in the area of sexuality,
but in every area of life. Am I doing this in His name or in my
own? Would God even want to associate Himself with what I'm
doing? Ultimately, is God glorified through this? So, in terms of
passion, someone who is trying to please God shouldn't be asking how close to the edge he or she can go before crossing the
line. A Christian should be more concerned with how close he or
she can get to God.

"So whether you eat or drink or whatever you do, do it all for
the glory of God."
(1 Cor. 10:31 NIV)

"And whatever you do, whether in word or deed, do it all in
the name of the Lord Jesus, giving thanks to God the Father
through him."
(Col. 3:17 NIV)

I am not of the school that discourages any physical interaction whatsoever (unless God has specifically given you that personal conviction). In my own experience you can have a certain amount of limited physical affection (hand-holding, arm around the shoulder, etc.), and through it you can actually experience God's love and joy. Our loving Father has given us the ability to enjoy one another's presence, and part of that joy is expressed through physical touch—done in a godly way! But be very careful that what is going on in your actions and in your thoughts is pure. If you have a prior experience of falling in the physical area, be very cautious, set up and stick to your boundaries, and don't put yourself in vulnerable situations.

Foremost in your mind must be the commitment to glorify Jesus in all circumstances. You and I must remember that God is watching and we will one day have to account for everything we have done. Living to please our Lord above all else should be our primary concern, both now and for all eternity. There are eternal consequences for our actions, but there are also consequences of sin in this life.

> "Nothing in all creation can hide from him. Everything is naked and exposed before his eyes. This is the God to whom we must explain all that we have done."
> (HEB. 4:13 NLT)

WHAT WOULD MY FUTURE SPOUSE THINK?

The second question we must ask ourselves is this: what would my future spouse think? I spoke to a young girl in her early twenties who said she cringed every time she thought about having to tell her future spouse about what she'd done with another guy. She said she hadn't wanted to fall sexually, but she did. She also said that the reason she was no longer a virgin was because she went past her boundaries and broke her standards. She thought that the little things weren't that big of a deal.

"Satan will tell you, 'There's nothing wrong with a little kiss. There's nothing wrong with touching and feeling,'" she said. "And then, he'll tell you there's nothing wrong with taking all your clothes off!"

At the Last Supper, Jesus told his disciple Peter, "Satan has asked to sift you as wheat" (Luke 22:31 NIV). He wants to sift you as well, causing you to allow first one compromise, then another to become permissible to you. If you have not clearly defined

Will you love me even when . . .

your boundaries, or if you choose not to stay within your boundaries, then one thing can lead to another.

For example, if you go through a mall and you have money but have made no prior decision to *not* buy something, you're probably going to buy things. Similarly, if you have a desire for someone and you feed that desire by overstepping your spiritual bounds, there's a good chance that you will fall.

Some people I have known have broken their standards after they met that "special someone," because they quickly abandoned the limits they had set for themselves when temptation came.

To be sure, Satan is the author of evil, and he will introduce temptation into our lives, yet James said, "Temptation comes from the lure of *our own* evil desires" (James 1:14 NLT, emphasis mine). When we fall into temptation, we cannot blame the devil for our reactions. We alone have the choice regarding our responses. James goes on to say, "These evil desires lead to evil actions, and evil actions lead to death" (v. 15). If we allow our "evil desires" to lead to "evil actions," then we will find ourselves, like the girl I mentioned earlier, cringing when we think of having to tell our future spouses that the gift of virginity was given to someone else.

"Do not share in the sins of others. Keep yourself pure."
(1 TIM. 5:22 NIV)

"But remember that the temptations that come into your life
are no different from what others experience. And God is

faithful. He will keep the temptation from becoming so strong that you can't stand up against it. When you are tempted, he will show you a way out so that you will not give in to it."

(1 COR. 10:13 NLT)

WHAT WOULD MY FUTURE CHILDREN THINK?

The last question we must think about when relating romantically to the opposite sex is this: what would my future children think? If you get married, most likely you are going to one day sit down with your kids and have the "birds and the bees" talk. In which position would you rather be? Do you want to have to say, "Honey, don't do what I did"? Or would you like to say, "I set some strong boundaries and stayed pure. Here is how you can stay pure too"? I know which situation I'd choose! I want my future children to be proud of how I conducted myself during the "hormone-infested years" and beyond.

Dr. James Dobson has said, "The best thing a father can do for his kids is to love their mother." In the same way, one of the gifts I can already be preparing for my future kids is my purity— showing them that I loved and respected their father by being faithful to him before I'd even met him.

"Real religion, the kind that passes muster before God the Father, is this: Reach out to the homeless and loveless in their plight, and guard against corruption from the godless world."

(JAMES 1:27 THE MESSAGE)

DON'T BUY THE LIE

Research has shown that one of the greatest pressures to have sex early doesn't come from love or lust but from peer pressure. Are you missing out? Or is God protecting you? Don't buy the lie from Satan that "everybody's doing it." Most high schoolers *haven't* had sex.

DID YOU KNOW . . . ?

- ❖ Over half of all high-school students have never had sex (51.6 percent).
- ❖ Seventy-eight percent of all fifteen-year-olds (73 percent of boys alone) have never had sex.
- ❖ If you add to the 78 percent those whose only sexual experience was involuntary, then about 84 percent of fifteen-year-olds have never had voluntary sex.
- ❖ Eighty-six percent of high-school girls (and 82 percent of boys) are not "sleeping around." Only 14 percent of high-school girls have had four or more sex partners.[1]
- ❖ The *Washington Times* reported that the trend toward abstinence is increasing, as evidenced by the number of "True Love Waits" commitments made each Valentine's Day.

I hope you see these qualities in me . . . .

_____
_____
_____
_____
_____
_____
_____
_____
_____
_____
_____
_____
_____
_____
_____
_____
_____

"Don't love the world's ways. Don't love the world's goods. Love of the world squeezes out love for the Father. Practically everything that goes on in the world—wanting your own way, wanting everything for yourself, wanting to appear important—has nothing to do with the Father. It just isolates you from him. The world and all its wanting, wanting, wanting is on the way out—but whoever does what God wants is set for eternity."

(1 John 2:15-17 The Message)

CONSEQUENCES

When it comes to consequences of wrong actions, I think many of us think like Scarlett O'Hara, the lead character in *Gone with the Wind*. Scarlett often said, "I'll think about it tomorrow." We often procrastinate for so long that by the time we start thinking about our own actions, it's too late—the deed is done. And all we're left with is regret.

Often we hear this statement from our society: "Do what you want unless it hurts someone else." That way of thinking is completely flawed. If you sin, if you don't glorify God with your actions, you will always hurt *somebody*. It could be you, your friends or family members, or your future spouse and children. But even if your sin doesn't affect another human being, it always hurts God. To avoid these consequences, the best way is simply to obey Him.

"It is God's will that you should be sanctified: that you should avoid sexual immorality; that each of you should learn to control his own body in a way that is holy and honorable, not in passionate lust like the heathen, who do not know God; and that in this matter no one should wrong his brother or take advantage of him. The LORD will punish men for all such sins, as we have already told you and warned you. For God did not call us to be impure, but to live a holy life."

(1 THESS. 4:3–7 NIV)

PHYSICAL CONSEQUENCES

More than 50 million Americans have been infected with STDs. Many teenagers believe that a condom will protect them from STDs. The truth is that having sex with condoms as your only means of "protection" is like playing with fire. Condoms fail one out of six times, and their packages even bear a disclaimer that they are no guarantee against disease. The National Institute of Health, the Centers for Disease Control and Prevention, the Food and Drug Administration, and other federal-government health agencies published a report that showed no data proving the effectiveness of condoms for preventing most sexually trans-mitted diseases.[2] Don't buy the lie of "safe sex" that this society feeds you. The only true safe sex is that within the context of marriage!

DID YOU KNOW . . . ?

❖ One in every four teenagers will be infected with a sexually transmitted disease (STD) before graduating from high school.

❖ Each day 33,000 Americans become infected with an STD, and 22,000 of these people are fifteen- to twenty-five-year-olds.

❖ Two STDs, human papillomavirus (a leading cause of cervical cancer) and chlamydia (the leading cause of infertility), are carried by at least one of every three teenage girls who have had sex.

❖ There are now more than fifty known STDs. Some of the diseases are itchy, burning, painful, and even deadly. Some of them can make you sterile. Some are incurable.[3]

One of my good friends told me about an acquaintance of hers who has a venereal disease. She said, "The emotional and physical pain that she suffers [from having multiple sex partners] is just such a high cost. Physically, she doesn't enjoy sex now with her husband because of the pain. The protection you have from diseases by only being with that one special person you marry is another way that God protects us through his design for marriage." Are you willing to risk a lifetime of good health for a few moments of pleasure?

Another obvious consequence of sex before marriage is that you might get pregnant. Every day 2,700 teens get pregnant.[4] Do the math—that's almost one million teenage girls becoming pregnant each year! Of that million, just over three in ten choose to abort the baby.[5] One in five teens that have sexual intercourse becomes pregnant. And yet most teenage girls think, *That could never happen to me! That happens to other people.* Take another look at the statistics. Are you willing to take the risk of totally changing the course of your future by making one mistake?

> "Don't be misled. Remember that you can't ignore God and get away with it. You will always reap what you sow! Those who live only to satisfy their own sinful desires will harvest the consequences of decay and death. But those who live to please the Spirit will harvest everlasting life from the Spirit."
>
> (GAL. 6:7–8 NLT)

EMOTIONAL CONSEQUENCES

Experiencing sex before marriage has emotional consequences that can bring lifelong pain. Some of these dangers are not immediately apparent. Many of them are hard to see until it's too late.

PAST REGRETS.

Many people experience deep sadness after engaging in sex before marriage. There is often the impression of being used and a feeling that you've given up something precious, and all for nothing. A majority of those who have had premarital sex do not end up marrying their first sexual partners. So many people express the sentiment, "I thought he [or she] really loved me!" But after the sexual encounter and the breakup of the relationship, the realization hits—"I guess it wasn't true love after all!" This feeling can last for years. It can cause severe emotional problems that will be carried into a marriage, damaging the feeling of intimacy that should exist between a husband and wife. Listen to one person's story:

> Because of our age and immaturity (I was fourteen and he was sixteen when we met), we didn't think about the consequences. I went into our relationship believing that I would not have sex before marriage, but we allowed ourselves to be in situations in which things could happen. It's like sticking your hand close to the fire; you're definitely going to get burned if you keep doing that. God was really trying to protect me—I see it now. If I could go back in time, I would not have had sex. The way God designs sex is very intricate. When you have sex outside of marriage, because God designed for it to bind two people together, the emotional stress, especially for me as a girl, was such a horrible thing. I was depressed and sad.

GUILT.

The feeling that you've done something wrong and can't forgive yourself can do severe damage to your self-image and influence how you respond to other relationships in your life. There is no sexual sin that God will not completely forgive if it is honestly confessed. (We'll talk more about that in chapter 6.) But the guilt that comes from sexual sin can haunt your heart for years, even when you *know* in your mind you are forgiven and declared "not guilty" by God. Satan will continue to throw your past mistakes in your face, and you may feel unworthy of God's love, or the love of another person. You may also experience guilt because of what you have done to others in taking something away from them, causing hurt, confusion, and emotional heartache. Listen to this wisdom from someone who knows:

> Even after we were married, I felt guilty whenever we had sex. I still associated being intimate with my now husband with feelings of guilt and sinfulness. For a while, I believed that because we had had sex prior to our wedding day that God would not bless our marriage. So I had a lot of anger, bitterness, and resentment toward my husband. Even though we were equally to blame, I was upset because he allowed it to happen. I really had to work through all this with God and my husband, and it took a long time.

FEAR OF COMMITMENT.

Although some people have sex "recreationally," most young people have sex because they are committed to someone and see it as a way of expressing their love. When that kind of relationship ends, the trust and ability to commit to someone else is often shattered. Once a person's heart is broken, fear of another broken commitment can hinder successful future relationships.

I have a friend who dated a girl for four years and then his girlfriend broke up with him. It has taken him another four years to get over that hurt enough to even try to be involved in another relationship—and they didn't have sex! Imagine how much greater his fear of commitment in future relationships would have been if he had given his virginity to her.

LOW SELF-ESTEEM.

People who have been used sexually are likely to have low self-esteem. Then to add insult to injury, many of these people begin to seek any kind of attention, even if it's in other harmful sexual relationships—all in a search for love and acceptance.

DESPAIR.

The emotional pain of losing your virginity, getting AIDS, contracting an STD, conceiving a baby outside of marriage, aborting that baby (or giving it to someone else), or destroying your reputation or someone else's can lead to severe hopelessness, depression, or even suicide. Satan will keep whispering, "It's over" or "There's no hope." Over and over again I've had people who attended my concerts tell me they've tried to commit suicide. More often than not, their despair stemmed from extreme feelings of rejection after giving themselves completely in sex outside of marriage.

SPIRITUAL CONSEQUENCES

Here are some practical reasons why a Christian should not have sex until marriage:

IT CAUSES YOU TO WITHDRAW FROM GOD.

Because of guilt, you may no longer feel you deserve to have a personal and intimate relationship with God. You may feel so ashamed of what you have done that you can't even approach Him in prayer. You may act like Adam and Eve in the Garden of Eden. After they sinned against Him, they ran and hid. But in those times when we hurt Him, that's when we need His reassurance the most!

IT IMPACTS YOUR WITNESS.

You are to be a mirror for Christ, and the sin in your life will block God's reflection. Many young adults have ruined their witnesses for Christ because of their actions. Grover Levy, a Christian musician, once penned the words, "If you want to lead me to Jesus, you better find a better way 'cause your life is speaking so loud I can't even hear a word you say."

IT LOWERS YOUR STANDARDS.

Good character includes decency, self-control, and respect for yourself and others. But if you experience sex before God intends for you to, you corrupt your character and degrade your own sexuality. Worse, after you've crossed the line, you've opened yourself up to a lot more temptations. Why? Because once you've gone beyond the physical boundaries you have set for yourself, it becomes easier to go a little further the next time. Pretty soon you've gone a lot further than you ever thought you would! And once you've fallen, it becomes easier to slip up again and again.

IT WILL AFFECT YOUR MARRIAGE.

Even if you think you're going to be spending the rest of your life with a person, don't have sex outside of marriage, because you will regret it. Contrary to some people's opinion, God didn't say it's OK to have sex if you're going to get married anyway. He knows the cost of that, and He knows what is best for us—to wait. Ultimately, if that person loves you, he or she will exercise patience and wait for you.

IT WILL CAUSE YOU PAIN.

A wise man once put it this way: "It is better to be innocent than forgiven." His point was that God can indeed wipe the slate clean, but you may carry the wounds of sin and pay the consequences of bad decisions for a lifetime. Even though from God's perspective we are "justified" (which means "just as if I'd never sinned"), from a practical standpoint the long-term effects may never go away. The emotional and spiritual pain will affect your walk with Christ, the spiritual intimacy you are meant to enjoy with your future spouse, and the way you view yourself. God wants you to be healthy—physically, emotionally, and spiritually.

If you take one piece of paper and glue it to another piece of paper, both pieces tear when you pull them apart. It is impossible to wind up with two papers that are as flawless as when you started. Because of the glue, each piece of paper is forever left with some parts from the other paper. That is exactly the way God designed sex. It is a physical union of two separate lives. Once the relationship becomes a unit (through physical, emotional, and spiritual intimacy), God intends for it to stay together. The intimacy that is part of the sexual act is so powerful, we must not take it lightly. Why take risks that can cause you pain the rest of your life? Your future marriage will be much happier if you don't have to deal with the negative physical, emotional, and spiritual consequences of sex before marriage.

BE AWARE OF THE POWER

First Timothy 4:2 talks about false teachers that would arise in the last days and lead people away from God. Paul describes them as "liars, whose consciences have been seared as with a hot iron." In other words, their consciences were *desensitized* to their sin. It is possible to commit certain sins so much and so often

I will wait for you because . . .

_____

_____

_____

_____

_____

_____

_____

_____

_____

_____

_____

_____

_____

_____

_____

_____

that you become desensitized to them. This is especially true of sexual sin. It is extremely powerful, and if you give in to it, repeating the sin becomes easier each time.

God made sex to be wonderful, joyful, uniting, beautiful, and good. But outside of marriage it can be exactly the opposite—a sad, cheap, damaging, loveless, and disappointing rendition of the real thing. Don't settle for the agony; wait for the ecstasy of sex God's way.

> "There's more to sex than mere skin on skin. Sex is as much spiritual mystery as physical fact. As written in Scripture, 'The two become one.' Since we want to become spiritually one with the Master, we must not pursue the kind of sex that avoids commitment and intimacy, leaving us more lonely than ever—the kind of sex that can never 'become one.' There is a sense in which sexual sins are different from all others. In sexual sin we violate the sacredness of our own bodies, these bodies that were made for God-given and God-modeled love, for 'becoming one' with another. Or didn't you realize that your body is a sacred place, the place of the Holy Spirit? Don't you see that you can't live however you please, squandering what God paid such a high price for? The physical part of you is not some piece of property belonging to the spiritual part of you. God owns the whole works. So let people see God in and through your body."
>
> (1 Cor. 6:17–20 The Message)

Father, when I think about the physical consequences of sex outside of marriage, it's scary. I see that Your plan for "safe sex" is within the protection of marriage and true love—and true love will wait for me! Help me to think about the consequences of sexual sin whenever temptations come my way. Help me to not put myself in vulnerable situations. I want to draw closer to You, and not be running and hiding from You in guilt and shame. I need You. I love You.

In the awesome name of Jesus, Amen.

Protecting Purity

I received a powerful story about the importance of prayer during this waiting process. Listen to Ian's inspirational testimony:

Arlene, my beautiful and faithful wife of twenty-five years, waited for me. As a young lady she would pray for her husband-to-be. I met her parents two years before I met her and knew them as the kind of Christian parents I never had.

While we were courting, Arlene and I talked about the challenges in our lives. It was absolutely amazing to hear about the times when she would be burdened to pray for her future husband and I was going through great difficulties. I always wondered who was praying for me during those times because I believe in prayer and in interceding before the throne of God. Please continue to encourage people to wait on the Lord and pray for the power of God to be made manifest in their relationships, both present and future.

CHAPTER four

Protecting Purity:

PRACTICAL WAYS TO WAIT IN A CULTURE THAT SCREAMS, "JUST DO IT!"

> Darling did you know I dream about life together
> Knowing it will be forever
> I'll be yours and you'll be mine

ENJOY THE WAIT

Every now and then, when I'm feeling a little lonely for my "some-one," I get in an extremely sappy, romantic mood. I dream about the simple things, like having someone to dress up for, someone to give me flowers, someone with whom to share my heart completely. It makes the waiting fun, to daydream like that. Waiting for your "darling" does not have to be boring, dull, or even free of romance.

I've heard people say that the anticipation of an experience is a large part of the joy of the experience itself. I believe this is often true. Not that marriage itself isn't going to be a blast—it will be! But part of enjoying marriage *then* is enjoying the waiting and dreaming *now*. So what are some things you can do now while you're waiting that will prepare you for the future? Let's take a look at a few ideas.

DARE TO DREAM

I think we've already covered this one.

PRACTICE UNSELFISHNESS

This is a biggie. It seems to me from everything I've ever heard about marriage that selfishness is the biggest and hardest issue to overcome—sounds like life, doesn't it? I know from watching my parents over the years that marriage involves struggling, giving, learning, saying "I'm sorry," serving when you don't feel like it, and a host of other things, in that "happily ever after." The bright side is that we can practice unselfishness and giving here and now with our families and friends.

Here are some practical ways to practice unselfishness and giving now:

- Clean the kitchen as a surprise for your mom.
- Play with your little brother or sister (even if you don't feel like it).
- Offer to make a cup of hot chocolate, tea, or coffee for your mom, dad, or sibling.
- Mow the yard without being asked.
- Give a card to a friend, sharing how you appreciate him or her.
- Observe others' needs and help meet them.
- Let others go first.
- Practice tidiness (guys, put the toilet seat down!).
- Don't always give your opinion—listen.
- Ask caring questions about others' lives.
- Practice taking responsibility for your actions.
- If you make a mess, clean it up. Don't expect someone else to do your work.

"It is obvious what kind of life develops out of trying to get your own way all the time: repetitive, loveless, cheap sex; a stinking accumulation of mental and emotional garbage; frenzied and joyless grabs for happiness; trinket gods; magic-show religion; paranoid loneliness; cutthroat competition; all-consuming-yet-never-satisfied wants; a brutal temper; an impotence to love or be loved; divided homes and divided lives; small-minded and lopsided pursuits; the vicious habit of depersonalizing everyone into a rival; uncontrolled and uncontrollable addictions . . ."

(GAL. 5:19–21 THE MESSAGE)

GROW STRONG FRIENDSHIPS

Do you want to know how to not be so lonely while you're waiting for "the one"? Invest in relationships with friends of the opposite sex. Not only will it help you realize that you're not facing the world alone, but you will also learn from those relationships. I believe that just through having friendships with members of the opposite sex you can discover some of the things you want and don't want in a future spouse. As you see the values and priorities of different people, you'll get a picture of the kind of things you're looking for in the person you want to marry. You'll also gain some great insight on interacting with the opposite sex and learning how to appreciate the differences of others.

WORK ON YOUR FAMILY RELATIONSHIPS

If you've got a great relationship with your brothers, sisters, and parents, that's awesome! It's probably because you've invested time in getting to know your family and being friends with them. Hopefully you've learned much about the art of giving to your family, which is great practice for marriage. But if you're like most people and would say that your family relationships need a lot of work, then some changes can be made.

Spend time with each individual family member, asking (and really caring) about what is going on in his or her life. The way you treat your family now is a good representation of how you will one day treat your spouse and children. What a great opportunity to work out the bugs and bad habits now!

> "So, chosen by God for this new life of love, dress in the wardrobe God picked out for you: compassion, kindness, humility, quiet strength, discipline. Be even-tempered, content with second place, quick to forgive an offense. Forgive as quickly and completely as the Master forgave you. And regardless of what else you put on, wear love. It's your basic, all-purpose garment. Never be without it."
> (COL. 3:12–14 THE MESSAGE)

ASK QUESTIONS AND READ BOOKS ABOUT PREPARING FOR MARRIAGE

If you're younger than sixteen, you probably don't even need to begin to think about reading books on marriage. But if you're above that age, you can start preparing for a great marital relationship by reading about what it takes to build a godly marriage.

I hope you are waiting for me because . . .

Regardless of your age, asking questions of godly people you respect is always a good idea. There is so much we can learn about any area in life from people who have gone before us. Ask your parents, grandparents, youth pastor, or other Christian adults who are truly living for Jesus. Even if your parents haven't been so successful in their marriage, gently ask them about what they've learned (maybe the hard way) about marriage.

SPEND QUALITY TIME WITH JESUS

The greatest way to live life well and to prepare for the future (marriage or no marriage) is to spend time with Jesus. A friend of mine told me that after she got married it was quite a challenge to maintain a regular devotional time because so much of her time was taken up in giving to her husband. It became even more difficult after having kids. And this is someone who had regular devotions before marriage. Imagine if she hadn't been as disciplined *then*—devotions *now* would be nonexistent.

Too many believers allow their spouses to take the place of God. God wants us to cherish our life partners, but He wants to be in first place in our lives. You can set that priority now, before you get married. Find your contentment in God by really seeking Him. If you don't find contentment, then you're going to expect your future spouse to fill those areas in your life that only God can fill. Create a regular pattern of meeting with Jesus every day in the Bible, worship, and prayer. Do you want to be the best spouse ever someday? Then meet with the greatest Man who ever lived *every* day! If you find your ultimate meaning and fulfillment in Christ, it will keep you from trying to find substitutes through sexual attention now. And it will take a tremendous amount of pressure off the marriage in the future.

> "Steep your life in God-reality, God-initiative, God-provisions. Don't worry about missing out. You'll find all your everyday human concerns will be met.
>
>   "Give your entire attention to what God is doing right now, and don't get worked up about what may or may not happen tomorrow. God will help you deal with whatever hard things come up when the time comes."
>
> (Matt. 6:33–34 The Message)

STAY ACTIVE

We used to have a commercial on television in Australia that showed several active people biking, hiking, running, flying kites, and playing various sports. Then the commercial switched to a scene showing a "couch potato." The catchphrase at the end was, "Life . . . be in it."

Don't pine about the house waiting for your prince (or princess) to come along! God made this world, this life, for us to enjoy, and subsequently praise Him for. Let's enjoy it! No matter who you are or what your situation, I can say with confidence that God intends for your life to be more than just a search for a spouse. Get busy with all He has for you!

LET GOD DEVELOP YOUR CHARACTER

You may truly believe that you are meant to be married—but God may have some things He wants to teach you, some ways He wants to see you grow—before you take that step. For one, He may be teaching you to wait patiently on Him.

It takes faith to walk in obedience when you feel as if God is not answering your prayers in the way you think He should, but God can use this period of waiting to develop godly characteristics in you, like kindness and self-control. Take a look at the fruit of the Spirit listed in Galatians 5:22–23 and ask yourself which fruits need to be grown more in your life. If you spend time with Him in prayer on a regular basis, He will show you what's in your heart and where you need to improve. Thank Him for this time and this opportunity for growth, and take full advantage of it!

> "So make every effort to apply the benefits of these promises to your life. Then your faith will produce a life of moral excellence. A life of moral excellence leads to knowing God better. Knowing God leads to self-control. Self-control leads to patient endurance, and patient endurance leads to godliness."
>
> (2 PETER 1:5–6 NLT)

ACHING TO BE HELD

Rather than protecting their purity and enjoying the wait, there are those who decide that their need for attention is greater than their need for a relationship with God.

During my teen years, I had a friend whom I will call "Julie," to respect her privacy. She and I had been distant friends but became closer at a youth camp. Through all the group sessions, meals, and off-the-wall games, we hung out a lot. But at night (when we were supposed to be going to sleep) we would talk.

One night I distinctly remember her asking me if I ever really longed for someone to hold me. She had come from a broken home, and she told me that sometimes she felt so lonely that she just ached to be held. During camp, she always seemed to be hanging out with the guys, and very much enjoyed their attention. But it still surprised me how deeply she was hurting and how needy she was. We fell out of contact when she went away to college.

Some time later I ran into her at a grocery store during one of her university breaks. Immediately I could see a difference in her, a sadness in her eyes. During the course of our conversation, she told me that she was pregnant. It came as quite a surprise to me since as far as I knew she had been a virgin until she went off to college.

Just the other day I was with my family at Cracker Barrel, and I saw her son, now five years old. He was with his grandparents

74

since she was at work. Julie had so many dreams of being a doctor, getting married, and having children. She told me once that though she doesn't regret her son, she does regret the fact that because of sex outside of marriage, her son is being raised without a father, and she is still alone.

> "So roll up your sleeves, put your mind in gear, be totally ready to receive the gift that's coming when Jesus arrives. Don't lazily slip back into those old grooves of evil, doing just what you feel like doing. You didn't know any better then; you do now. As obedient children, let yourselves be pulled into a way of life shaped by God's life, a life energetic and blazing with holiness. God said, 'I am holy; you be holy.'"
> (1 Peter 1:13–16 The Message)

BE SMART

A guy wrote to me and said, "The idea of waiting until marriage for sex is wonderful, but one has to also consider the complete devastation that can come if something unexpected happens." He was referring to rape. Even though his approach was quite negative in thought, his message and subsequent warning is very important. I have heard stories of girls whose lives ended up being ravaged by rape just by taking a walk across a park alone at night. All it takes is a few minutes in the wrong place at the wrong time and your whole life could be changed forever.

We can't completely guarantee that our virginity will not be taken from us, but we can commit to being "shrewd as snakes and as innocent as doves" (Matthew 10:16 NIV). Walking alone at night is never a good idea. In today's fallen world, a class in self-defense is wise. Girls, be careful not to be in a closed room with a guy you do not know well. Even walking during the day in unpopulated places can be dangerous. And, guys, you're not completely immune from the problem of rape either. First Peter 5:8 says, "Be careful! Watch out for attacks from the Devil, your great enemy. He prowls around like a roaring lion, looking for some victim to devour" (NLT). The old adage "better safe than sorry" has never been more relevant.

If you were the victim of rape or molestation, be assured that God still honors your commitment to remain pure. You did not voluntary give up your virginity, and God knows the circumstances. In the area of sexual purity, you are completely clean and innocent in His sight. Thank God that in His grace He can bring healing to you. And although it is very difficult, He can even lead you to forgive the one who abused you.

FIND A MENTOR

Another way to busy yourself in this time of waiting is to find a mentor. A mentor is someone who is a trusted counselor or guide, a tutor or coach, someone who has "been there" and can provide wise counsel for the road ahead.

I trust in God's plan for me because . . .

My grandmother is one of my mentors. She is seventy-five years old and one of the most gentle, beautiful, and loving people I know. My grandpa died about eight years ago, and since then my grandma and I have taken many trips together. We've gone to the beach, to a bed-and-breakfast, and soon we hope to visit England together. Apart from simply enjoying her company, one of the big reasons I want to hang out with her is to be influenced by her. I want her to "rub off" on me.

I have often admired the respect that Chinese young people show their elders. They are taught to hold in very high regard the wisdom that their parents and grandparents have earned.

Unfortunately, in latter years (largely due to the influence of Western culture) many Chinese-American young people have chosen to abandon the traditional values of their parents and grandparents and have turned their backs on morality. Their parents have preached modesty and a conservative lifestyle, but they live in a culture that is anything but modest! Both girls and guys often feel as though they are caught between their parents' customs and the lifestyles they see in other American teens.

In times past (even though it wasn't always called "mentoring"), the respect Chinese young people had for their elders and the amount of time they spent together prevented a lot of problems. Order and morality were preserved because of the wisdom given through mentoring.

But today, as less and less youth look to mentors for guidance, more and more trouble has resulted. The rise of Asian-Americans joining gangs indicates a search for identity on the part of some who reject their parents' values and look for belonging elsewhere. And though sexual activity is less common among Chinese teens than among American youth, the rate is rising. These youths desperately need the godly influence that mentoring can provide.

Mentoring can be a powerful thing in all cultures. It is an art form that has been lost in recent generations, but needs to be restored. Begin it again in your generation. Ask your mom, dad, uncle, aunt, or grandparent to mentor you. You could also ask an older person of the same sex from your church. Listen to their "life stories." Study together. Pray together. You will be amazed by what you will learn!

> "Guide older women into lives of reverence so they end up as neither gossips nor drunks, but models of goodness. By looking at them, the younger women will know how to love their husbands and children, be virtuous and pure, keep a good house, be good wives. We don't want anyone looking down on God's Message because of their behavior. Also, guide the young men to live disciplined lives."
>
> (Titus 2:3–6 The Message)

WISE COUNSEL

My grandparents and mentors, Geoff and Jean Francis, are now fifty-five years into marriage! They laugh and tease each other and really enjoy life together. I recently asked them for their wisdom on a variety of subjects concerning relationships. Here's how our conversation went:

REBECCA: What advice can you give on guy-girl relationships that this generation of young people should know?

NANNA [JEAN]: Sex wasn't really talked about in our day, but it definitely is now. Sex is sacred—don't let too much free action, free talk, or public displays of affection into your relationship. There is a fine line between purity and sexual liberty. Our bodies are the temple of God. If we abuse the sacred gift of sex, then we are really abusing God's beautiful gift to us.

POP [GEOFF]: First, let your relationship proceed slowly in courting and engagement. Second only to your relationship with God, marriage (and whom you choose to marry) is vitally important. The decisions you make affect not only you and your possible spouse, but also your future family and others around you.

NANNA: Don't isolate yourselves as a couple. Get together in groups, because in that way you become friends. There comes a time eventually for being alone together, but don't have too much time too soon. Another benefit of getting together in groups is that you can really be yourself and get the other person to be himself (or herself) as well.

POP: Be friends before romance. Don't be "unequally yoked" spiritually (i.e., don't date someone who doesn't share your faith); have a spiritual foundation in your relationship, for it is the rock of a long-lasting marriage. It's also important to know the background of the family you're considering marrying into.

> "Do not be yoked together with unbelievers. For what do righteousness and wickedness have in common? Or what fellowship can light have with darkness?"
> (2 Cor. 6:14 NIV)

Dating (or courting) someone who is not a Christian is never a good idea. Even if you think you can "change" or "convert" that person, the Bible says no. More often than not, he or she will bring you down rather than you influencing him or her in a positive way. You don't want to run the risk of this person "making a commitment" and find out later that it was all a pretense—just to win you. Let God draw that person. Why would you want to consider spending your life with someone who doesn't understand the deepest part of your heart? The bond we have in Jesus is the most sacred, uniting bond of all.

Note: On knowing the background of a potential spouse's family, it has been said that you don't just marry a *person*; rather, you marry that person *plus* his or her parents, grandparents, sisters, or brothers—the whole family! It's true. If you don't get along with your boyfriend's mother now, it might not get better after you marry. Is she jealous of your relationship with her son? It is not likely to change. Guys, do you have conflict with your girlfriend's sister or brother? That conflict may continue after marriage. Do parents or grandparents interfere with your relationship now? They may interfere with your marriage.

An old adage says that a woman can tell how she will be treated in marriage by observing how her future husband treats his mother. Although that is not always the ironclad truth, it bears consideration. Does the young man speak condescendingly or disrespectfully to his mother? He will probably do the same to you. Guys, how does the girl you want to marry regard her father? Is she rebellious and rude? She may not have respect for the male gender.

WHAT IF NO ONE EVER COMES?

I've been asked numerous times when talking about waiting for the special guy or girl God has for you, "What if marriage, and therefore sex, is not in God's plan for me? What if God *doesn't* have someone special waiting for me?"

I don't pretend to have all the answers, but I *do* serve a God who does. Even though this is an extremely tough thing to deal with if you don't feel God has called you to a life of singleness, your best option is to put your trust in God, realizing He doesn't make mistakes. David wrote, "Delight yourself in the LORD and he will give you the desires of your heart" (Ps. 37:4 NIV). The Word also says, "Your Father knows what you need before you ask him"

I made a resolution about you today . . .

(Matt. 6:8). Be assured that God always has your best interests at heart. (For more on this question, see chapter 7.)

I've known people who have gotten married to someone out of fear of loneliness, or purely for sexual reasons. The results can be disastrous! Proverbs 21:9 says, "Better to live on a corner of the roof than share a house with a quarrelsome wife" (NIV). An older married friend recently said to me, "It is better to be single than to wish you were." As a single person, I struggle with times of loneliness, but so do married people! Whether God has called us to be married or single, it really comes down to the same thing—making Him our first love, focusing our gazes on Him.

> "Sometimes I wish everyone were single like me—a simpler life in many ways! But celibacy is not for everyone any more than marriage is. God gives the gift of the single life to some, the gift of married life to others.
>
> "I do, though, tell the unmarried and widows that singleness might well be the best thing for them, as it has been for me. But if they can't manage their desires and emotions, they should by all means go ahead and get married. The difficulties of marriage are preferable by far to a sexually tortured life as a single."
>
> (1 COR. 7:7-9 THE MESSAGE)

Lord Jesus, help me to enjoy this season of waiting and dreaming about my future spouse! Thank You for blessing me with awesome friends and family members to help in this waiting process. Thank You for the mentors You have placed in my life. Teach me now what it means to be unselfish—to put others' needs ahead of mine. I want to enjoy the abundant life You have given me. Show me where I need to grow. Reveal to me Your heart. I desire all that You have for me.

I love You, Lamb of God.

In Your name, Amen.

Love and Marriage

One of the future joys I anticipate is giving myself in purity to my husband on my wedding day. Here is a touching story of a girl from Texas who joyfully looks forward to this as well:

> When I first heard about "waiting," it was at a youth conference at a church I visited. I prayed to God that day and promised Him and my future husband my mind, body, and spirit. That summer my family and I traveled to my dad's hometown to visit family and to go to the annual Fourth of July parade. In a little store downtown we found abstinence rings. There was a whole section full of them. I took my time in choosing a special one. My dad bought it for me. And there, outside the store, with people watching, I made the commitment vocal. I said proudly that I was waiting until marriage to give myself to a man. My dad got on

his knees and slipped the ring onto my finger. Tears glistened in my eyes and my dad openly cried. He hugged me, saying he was very proud of me for the decision I had made.

Now I'm seventeen years old, and that very ring is still on my finger. My commitment still stands. People ask me about the ring and what it symbolizes. I smile and tell them. Even though temptation is there, glaring me in the eye, I say no. My promise stays. God and my future husband deserve it. I don't know who God has planned for me, but I know he's there. And I pray for him every night. I'm still waiting.

CHAPTER *five*

Love and Marriage:

WHAT IT IS WE'RE WAITING FOR

> And darling when I say 'til death do us part
> I'll mean it with all of my heart
> Now and always faithful to you

MORE THAN A FEELING

My best friend, Karleen, is a sweet, sunny-natured, wonderful girl originally from Louisiana. I met her at youth group in 1995. I had prayed for a friend like her for years.

Karleen married her boyfriend of five years, Jason, at age eighteen. I was delighted to be a bridesmaid in her wedding. Karleen had asked me to write a song for her wedding, so I sang "I Will Stand by You," accompanied by her brother, Gary, on guitar.

From this hour until the end of time
My life is truly yours and yours is mine.
I pledge my love to you, these vows I'll keep.
I promise to be faithful through the years.

Stop, hear my heart,
I can't live without you.
What could tear us apart?
Stop, look and see, that I want to be with you
For eternity.

I will stand by you,
I will love you forever.
I will stand by you,
I commit to forever.

In this love we will live,
In joy we will give
To each other, my dearest friend.

These hands I give to you to serve you well.
This heart I place in yours like no one else.
And as we live and learn and grow to be one,
I know our Father will lead us on.

Stop, hear me out,
This means so much more to me
Than you could ever tell.
Stop, look and see, that I want to be with you
For eternity.

For richer, for poorer,
For better or worse.
I'll love you, I'll serve you
And I will never turn.[1]

I asked Karleen to share what each part of the traditional marriage vows means to her, now that she's been married for over six years. This is what she shared with me:

On my wedding day I was so happy and experiencing all those "gushy" feelings, but I knew that there were going to be hard days ahead, when those feelings wouldn't always be there. That's when the marriage vows come to life!

I take you to be my lawful wedded husband (He's my husband and he's always going to be my husband.)

To have and to hold (the pleasure that is in marriage, the sweet part of simply having a companion for life)

From this day forward (This marked the beginning of our journey of life together and we're not just individuals—we're a team.)

For better, for worse (Despite the hard times, and the moments I don't feel the love I should, I'm committed to my marriage and my husband.)

For richer, for poorer (Whether we have wealth or nothing, we're blessed because we have each other, we have our family.)

In sickness and in health (If he was sick, I would be by his side; nothing would change as far as my love for him.)

To love and to cherish (A friend's husband died just recently, and through this I learned not to take my husband for granted. It's the simple, small things that show how much you love and cherish your spouse.)

'Til death do us part (There are things that can be devastating and deadly for a marriage, but none of those things would cause me to want to part from my husband. I am committed to my husband until death.)

As God is my witness (Wow! That's a big one! God's hand is on this marriage—this is a sacred thing. God is the one who joined us together. This is His marriage, and to allow it to be broken would be to grieve Him.)

I give you my promise. (I gave him my word that day that I would be his for my whole life.)

> "Now that you have purified yourselves by obeying the truth so that you have sincere love for your brothers, love one another deeply, from the heart."
> (1 Peter 1:22 niv)

> "Honor marriage, and guard the sacredness of sexual intimacy between wife and husband. God draws a firm line against casual and illicit sex."
> (Heb. 13:4 The Message)

One of the true heroes in my life, Mother Teresa, once said this:

> "Each time anyone comes into contact with us, they must become different and better people because of having met us. We must radiate God's love. . . . Intense love does not measure . . . it just gives."

I included these vows in this book and what they mean to a married young woman for two reasons: first, so that you can see an example of a functional, loving, committed marriage; and second, so that you can realize the seriousness of the marriage commitment. Too many people today trivialize and take far too lightly the covenant of marriage. Read over the vows again and let both the beauty and the seriousness of marriage sink in.

WHAT WE'RE REALLY WAITING FOR

The common view of marriage is so incredibly off center. It is so far from being on target with what God planned that we need to find another reset button for ourselves, one that deals with our view of marriage. We have all been so affected by divorce, anger, separation, adultery, and downright disrespect for the covenant of marriage that we see all around us that it is no wonder that our image of true love is rather askew.

First Corinthians 13 has been hailed as the "love chapter" in Christian circles. It contains some of the Bible's best counsel on what true love looks like. God also gives us many examples of what true and pure *married* love should be. Here are a few awesome marriage verses:

> "Wives, understand and support your husbands by submitting
> to them in ways that honor the Master. Husbands, go all out
> in love for your wives. Don't take advantage of them."
> (COL. 3:18–19 THE MESSAGE)

> "You will submit to one another out of reverence for Christ.
> You wives will submit to your husbands as you do to the LORD.
> For a husband is the head of his wife as Christ is the head

of his body, the church; he gave his life to be her Savior. As the church submits to Christ, so you wives must submit to your husbands in everything. And you husbands must love your wives with the same love Christ showed the church. He gave up his life for her."

(EPH. 5:21–25 NLT)

"That is the way the holy women of old made themselves beautiful. They trusted God and accepted the authority of their husbands. . . . In the same way, you husbands must give honor to your wives. Treat her with understanding as you live together. She may be weaker than you are, but she is your equal partner in God's gift of new life. If you don't treat her as you should, your prayers will not be heard."

(1 PETER 3:5, 7 NLT)

The Bible paints a true picture of marriage through the example of Jesus, who laid down His life for His bride, the Church. Jesus demonstrated the ultimate model of love and protection for husbands. As the body of Christ, we are to rest in and submit to that protection. This gives us quite a different portrait than the world gives us, doesn't it? This world's view about relationships and marriage is all about "me, myself, and I." It feeds us a user mentality that says things like this: "If he pleases me, then I'll stay with him," or "If she serves me as she should, then we'll stick together." It is about conditional commitment and, ultimately, complete selfishness.

Have you ever dreamed about . . .

_____

_____

_____

_____

_____

_____

_____

_____

_____

_____

_____

_____

_____

_____

_____

_____

_____

_____

_____

_____

_____

The Bible gives us the absolute opposite view, one of giving up rights to self, of serving the other person. Want to learn a marriage secret that successful married couples all over the world would tell you? Your marriage will never be a happy one as long as you are just looking out for yourself. Over and over I have heard couples, including my own parents, say that their marriages only became great when they learned to give, love, and serve more than they sought to receive. This is a principle we can be practicing now because it is a life principle, not just one that applies to marriage. Whenever we choose to serve ourselves, selfishness—not to mention unhappiness—grows. But when we give our lives up completely to God, to love and serve Him and then others, joy reigns in our hearts.

> "If you cling to your life, you will lose it; but if you give it up for me, you will find it."
> (MATT. 10:39 NLT)

A GREAT LOVE

My dad has often told me that when he got married he thought it was going to be one everlasting honeymoon. He said that he had a glamorous view of marriage because his parents never fought (at least in front of him). So when marriage wasn't the nonstop fun fest he thought it was going to be, he started to read marriage book after marriage book, searching for the problem.

He finally found a book called *Inside Out* by Larry Crabb that turned his perspective around. It taught him the importance of loving unconditionally without thought of return. And Mum responded to his unconditional love, and their marriage got better and better.

My dad will now tell anyone (and he does!), "I'm more infatuated with my wife than I've ever been." Their love is an inspiration to me, and I hope to have a similar "great love" someday. My dad also shared that though it's worth every minute of it, it's hard work. He said, "Marriage was a shock because I realized how selfish I was." It takes a lot of effort to have a great love.

> "You, my brothers, were called to be free. But do not use your
> freedom to indulge the sinful nature; rather, serve one
> another in love."
> (GAL. 5:13 NIV)

Here's a little about a couple who worked very hard at their great love and were rewarded for their efforts:

A Severe Mercy, by Sheldon Vanauken, is a real-life love story of a non-Christian couple who decided they wanted to make their love last and began to search for ways to do so. Throughout the process they became Christians and became friends with one of the greatest Christian minds ever, C. S. Lewis. I've drawn such inspiration from this book, and parts of it have become a road map for how I want my marriage to be. One of the principles they adopted, to attempt to keep alive their "inloveness," was sharing everything.

> We talked deeply . . . about how to make love endure. What emerged from our talk was nothing less, we believed, than the central "secret" of enduring love: sharing. "Look," we said. "What is it that draws two people into closeness and love?" Of course there's the mystery of physical attraction, but beyond that it's the things they share. . . . That way we shall create a thousand strands, great and small, that will link us together.[2]

The secret of their romantic love was deep communion, one feeling connected with the other. We can apply that same principle to our everyday relationships now, and from those friendships draw strength to wait. I'm not necessarily referring to romantic relationships; I'm thinking of parents, brothers, sisters, and close friends of the same sex. The power is in the sharing, the connectedness. I believe there would be a lot less sexual immorality if there wasn't such a sense of being "alone against the world" in the hearts of so many young people.

The other thing that Sheldon and his wife, "Davy," discovered was that "the killer of love is creeping separateness. Taking love for granted. . . . Ceasing to do things together. Finding separate interests. 'We' turning into 'I.' Self. Self-regard: what *I* want to do. . . ."

This is what I imagine you will be like . . .

We can embrace and practice these principles in our relationships now, and it helps us to wait because we don't feel alone!

WHAT TO LOOK FOR

While you're waiting for that "great love" to come into your life, here are some characteristics that I'm looking for in my future mate and I believe are traits we all need to seek in a future spouse. By the way, these would be good traits for you and me to develop in our own lives as well:

- ❖ gentleness
- ❖ a servant's heart
- ❖ patience
- ❖ a joyful spirit
- ❖ purposefulness
- ❖ loyalty and faithfulness
- ❖ passion for God
- ❖ a giving spirit
- ❖ unselfishness
- ❖ a hopeful heart
- ❖ kindness
- ❖ openness and honesty

> "The Lord does not look at the things man looks at. Man looks
> at the outward appearance, but the Lord looks at the heart."
> (1 Sam. 16:7 niv)

MOTHERLY ADVICE

What does a biblical marriage look like? Since the best model of marriage I've seen has been that of my parents, I recently interviewed my mum about her thoughts on marriage. Here is what she had to say:

Q: What advice would you give young people that you wish you'd known before you were married?

A: Take relationships slowly. Today's culture is a very sexual culture. Our fallen nature always wants to flirt with being a bit naughty, a bit on the edge. Take that and add to it the movies and the TV shows we watch, and it makes us want to know what it feels like. Because we've seen it demonstrated a certain way, you've got to take an active stance on taking it slowly physically. Set some boundaries and rules that can help grow the relationship gradually.

Don't date too young. If you're not in a position to marry within three or so years, then you're probably too young to date.

To get to know someone, you need to see him or her in a normal environment. You need to see the person with his or her family and this person needs to see you with yours. In your home you're more relaxed and less likely to put on a front. Observe the relationships within the family; watch how they relate to each other.

In getting to know someone, it's important to talk a lot. Talking helps develop friendships; it helps you to get inside someone else's head. Good communication leads to a strong foundation for marriage.

Q: What did the marriage vows mean to you on your wedding day?

A: When you get married, I don't think you tend to think about all that the vows represent, except that you do know that you're making a lifelong commitment. And that's scary, because you don't know what life's going to bring you. Because of the fear of the unknown, for me to make those vows and have peace I had to know that this person was God's choice for my life.

When I stood there and said those vows, in the back of my mind was the assurance that "All things work together for good to those who love God, to those who are called according to his purpose" [Rom. 8:28]. Because of that, I could trust God for the future.

You don't know whether you will end up being well off or living in a shack; you don't know whether your spouse will have an accident and become a quadriplegic, or have a nervous breakdown. Regardless of what the future deals you, you are committing to love this person through it all. How you could do it without the strong foundation of Jesus, I don't know!

"FOR RICHER FOR POORER, IN SICKNESS AND IN HEALTH"

Q: How do you know that a person is God's will for your life?

A: Pray about your relationship—hand it to God! Say to Him, "God, I love this person, but I want to know what *You* think." You even have to be prepared to let go of the relationship if you feel that God says, "No!" In giving the relationship to God completely, it takes it beyond human desire and attraction. This "giving it all to God" places the relationship on a very strong foundation because during times of disappointment and trouble you can say, "This person is God's will for my life, so I'm going to work through the problems with His strength."

> "We plan the way we want to live, but only God makes us able to live it."
> (Prov. 16:9 The Message)

> "I know, Lord, that a person's life is not his own. No one is able to plan his own course."
> (Jer. 10:23 nlt)

This abandonment to God keeps the relationship, the love, from being ruined by becoming possessive. When someone chooses to become selfish and "smother" someone else, the love never grows or matures—it dies. True love is not selfish; it never makes a possession of that other person. Rather, true love is a sharing of lives together.

The second step is to receive confirmation from God as to whether or not the person is God's will for your life. In our case, God confirmed His will through other people in our lives, people we respected spiritually, as they affirmed the relationship. I had been praying specifically for confirmation, and on separate occasions two older people encouraged me. God can use many ways to confirm His will. Some of these ways also include His speaking to you during your Bible reading and private devotions, your prayer time, and through family members and Christian friends who know you best.

Q: What advice can you give after twenty-seven years of marriage?

A: Keep open communication—no secrets!

Be vulnerable; allow your partner to see your heart, to see inside you.

Kindle romance.

Do things together, even little day-to-day things.

Be involved in each other's interests, even if you're not very interested. Find something to like!

Laugh—find the funny side of things.

Share one another's experiences during the day.

Give the other person the benefit of the doubt.

Set aside time just to be together—and protect that time!

Focus on serving one another.

Love is more than words; express love in action.

Sacrificially give. Give to your mate in a way that is difficult for you, but that he or she enjoys. This will express your deep love for him or her. Do the hard things, the things that *you* find hard to do but that you know your partner would like you to do.

"TO LOVE AND TO CHERISH"

My mum is awesome—I don't know what I'd do without her insight and practical advice! By practicing faithfulness and commitment now, you are preparing for your future relationships, whether that includes marriage or a life of singleness devoted to God. Realize that when you vow to stay sexually pure until marriage, you are staying faithful to that person *now* when you haven't even met the one God has for you. Faithfulness within marriage will be so much easier when you have practiced it outside of marriage. Ask God to continue to help you exercise faithfulness, and to develop in you a servant's heart, one that loves unconditionally, without thought of what you will get in return. In the big things and the small things of your life, God will show you how He wants to mature you as you seek His perfect plan for your present and your future. And the end result of that is definitely worth waiting for!

I'll need you to help me with . . .

Jesus, King of my heart, You have shown me the greatest example of what a true marriage looks like. Help me to learn from the ultimate model . . . You. I surrender my plans. I place them at Your feet. I trust You with my future.

I pray for my future spouse, if that is in Your plan for my life. May my future mate remain pure. Thank You for the example of true love You have expressed to me.

In Your wonderful name, Amen.

A Second Chance

God is a God of forgiveness, a God of second chances. This is an inspiring story from a mother of the bride that is full of hope in the face of loss:

> *My daughter was just recently married. We used your song, "Wait for Me," during a multimedia presentation before the ceremony began. We showed pictures from the lives of my daughter and her husband as the music played. My daughter loves the song because it speaks of a second chance. That was very important to both of them.*
>
> *Three weeks before the wedding, a tornado came through our area and destroyed my future son-in-law's house, with lots of the wedding decorations and gifts inside and the rings! (Eventually the rings were*

found—that was a miracle!—and some of the wedding decorations were salvaged.)

I know that God was present because our son-in-law was at work. My daughter had planned on being there to fix up the house but had been scheduled to work (she almost never worked on Mondays). Had they been home, they would have been killed.

Even though the whole tornado ordeal was devastating, it really did provide a fresh start for them both. It cleared out the clutter and some bad, regrettable memories.

One thing that was saved from the devastation was Rebecca's TRANSFORM CD. It had never been taken out of my daughter's car.

An article appeared in our local paper that expressed surprise that they were going to follow through with the wedding even after losing almost everything they owned. They were able to show that God was in control of the situation.

The wedding was a beautiful celebration of an old-fashioned courtship. Our son-in-law asked permission to court our daughter, then, before he asked her to marry him, he asked for our blessing. I had prayed for my daughter's future husband from the time I was saved (she was only four years old). When I told Daniel that if he was the one who married Stephanie, then I had been praying for him for the past sixteen years, he was taken aback—and then he thanked me. When he did propose, he did it before our church family of three hundred. Yes, girls, there still are guys like that out there. You just have to wait for them!

CHAPTER *six*

A Second Chance:

FORGIVENESS AND HOPE FOR THE GUILT-RIDDEN AND HURTING

> Now I know you may have made mistakes
> But there's forgiveness and a second chance
> So wait for me, darling, wait for me, wait for me . . .

YOU ARE LOVED

Every time I discuss the issue of sexual purity, I see it as extremely important to also talk about forgiveness. A couple of years ago a young girl was brought backstage to share her story with me. With tears she told me that she had been dating a guy for a while when he started to pressure her to have sex with him. For a time she resisted and said no. Eventually, though, she gave in and they had sex.

A week after they slept together for the first time, he broke up with her. She was completely devastated. She could not understand why he would do this to her, so she went to him and asked him why. He answered that the only reason that he had slept with her was because he wanted to make sure that he didn't love her. Can you believe that he would actually say that?

This young girl was so shattered that she got involved with drugs and alcohol and slept with many guys after that. She showed me the marks on her arm where she had tried to commit suicide. Her message to me was basically, "Don't let people go through what I have been through—warn them of the consequences of sex outside of marriage."

She was so broken by what had happened that I could see it through her story, her eyes, and her tears. I shared with her that if she had asked Jesus for forgiveness, then she was new, clean, whole. I strongly felt led to write on her hand in black marker, "I am loved." Every day I told her to look at her hand and believe that it is true. And now that the words have faded, I hope that she still looks at her hand and remembers.

"But God showed his great love for us by sending Christ to die for us while we were still sinners."
(Rom. 5:8 nlt)

FORGIVENESS IS NOT AN OPTION

Recently I spoke with two friends of mine who had some really good things to say about the issue of forgiveness. I will call this couple "Rob and Sandy" to respect their privacy. Rob shared with me that he didn't become a Christian until he was twenty-six years old. Unfortunately, he made many mistakes in the area of sexual immorality before becoming a believer. Now he is very happily married with three great kids, and he's in the ministry. I asked him to share his thoughts on sex and forgiveness. This is what he said:

> "First of all, the world has made sex too important. Even in marriage, too much emphasis is placed on it. I now realize that sex is not the biggest part of the intimacy of marriage—it is an extra blessing, but not the primary blessing. Forgiveness . . . is not an option. If we belong to Christ, then God has forgiven us, therefore we have no right to not forgive others, or ourselves.
>
> "People often talk about how sex outside of marriage affects us physically and spiritually, but I don't hear as much talk about the emotional consequences, such as guilt and self-esteem problems. By reminding me of my past mistakes, Satan tries to distract me, to deceive me and make me feel unworthy of God's love. At times like that I have to remember the truth of 2 Corinthians 10:5, 'We

demolish arguments and every pretension that sets itself up against the knowledge of God, and we take captive every thought to make it obedient to Christ' [NIV]. Every one of us has things that we regret in our pasts, but the thing that we need to keep in mind is that God is bigger than any obstacle we can face. Nothing is too big (or bad) for God's forgiveness. God can heal anyone."

One of the other things that Rob said was that in order to let God be Lord of our lives and really heal and renew us, we've got to take ourselves off the throne! When he said that, it really struck me that so often we try to equate God's ability to forgive with our own. It's almost as if, by not accepting God's power to forgive our sin, we are trying to decide—for God—what we will and won't forgive. How crazy is that?

> "He has removed our rebellious acts as far away from us as the east is from the west."
>
> (Ps. 103:12 NLT)

TURN IT OVER

Sandy had become a Christian in the fifth grade, but she strayed away and went through years of "doing her own thing" that included more than a few sexually intimate relationships. She had some very honest, but hopeful, things to say:

When you hang out with your friends do you . . .

_____

_____

_____

_____

_____

_____

_____

_____

_____

_____

_____

_____

_____

_____

_____

_____

_____

_____

"If you have had sex outside of marriage you're going to live with the scars—there are certain consequences to all of life's actions; that's why God tells us not to sin. But He *can* turn those things around and use them for good."

At first she felt as if she couldn't challenge people who were living the same lifestyle that she had lived because she had done the very same things she was challenging. But then she realized that God could really use her to point people in the right direction—an I've-been-where-you're-headed; -don't-go-there approach. She concluded her thoughts with these words: "I wish people could just realize that once they turn this area over to God, He'll take care of it. By turning it over to Him, God can then have control and He can bless them."

ACCEPT GOD'S HEALING

Months ago my editor, Dale Reeves, and I began the planning of this book on a cold, wintry night at Steak and Shake. I had just performed a Keith Green song called "Your Love Broke Through" at a Gospel Music Hall of Fame event. (Hey, it was late, and Steak and Shake was all that was open!) My dad, who is my manager, was there to help discuss the book, and a friend, whom I will call "Brooke," came along as well. She kept pretty quiet as we threw ideas around about what we thought the book should include. Later I found out that after leaving the restaurant she went home and cried her eyes out. Our discussion had struck a painful chord with her, and she felt that the book couldn't relate to her at all. You see, her virginity had been stolen away through the horror of sexual abuse.

That night ended up being a catalyst for Brooke to receive healing. She realized that because she had not willingly given away her virginity, in every respect other than the physical, she was still a virgin. She had never believed this up until that point. She so wholeheartedly embraced this new revelation that she ended up shocking even herself by telling her grandma that she was a virgin and was going to stay that way until after marriage. I'm so proud of her! She told me recently, "Because of the freedom and healing that comes from God, I know that in His sight I am pure, white as snow, precious, and I am a virgin."

"No matter how deep the stain of your sins, I can remove it. I can make you as clean as freshly fallen snow. Even if you are stained as red as crimson, I can make you as white as wool."

(Isa. 1:18 NLT)

FORGIVE THE HURT

This is a powerful testimony of a girl in college with whom I have kept in touch for quite some time:

"I was abused as a little girl by my uncle from the time I was ten until I was thirteen years old. I've only been dealing with my hurt the last few years. I've come to realize that I had built up all these walls for so long in an effort to try to hide the pain of the abuse. I've discovered that this cycle continues, and you build up walls in every area of your life. By trying to block out the pain, not only did I block out the bad feelings, but I also shut off the good feelings from my childhood as well. The thinking goes something like this: 'Don't let yourself feel anything and then you won't get hurt.'

"In order to deal with all this, one of the first things I had to do was admit to someone close to me that I had been abused. If you are in this situation, *you must find someone and tell your story.* The more you share with others about what happened to you, the less control it has over you, because the burden is shared. Then the pressure isn't all on you anymore.

"That's where I started. Finding a Christian counselor is also really important because you are able to share how you're feeling and then come to understand *why* you feel those things. After experiencing sexual abuse, you feel so alone, but when you open up and share the pain with others, you come to see that there are so many people struggling with the same feelings as yours. After you start processing the pain, you can begin to feel the opposite emotion of joy and happiness again.

"We all have a tendency to ask God for forgiveness and then take the weight of our sin back again. It's often like that with abuse as well. You think you've forgiven the person who has hurt you, but then the hurt comes back and you wonder if you were ever really able to forgive in the first place. When that happens to me, I pray that God will help me deal with the pain, forgive my uncle, and let go of it. One of the things that helps me to forgive is knowing that God has forgiven me for so much, so how then can I not forgive this man for hurting me? Just as my uncle's sin has hurt me, my sin hurts God and yet He still forgives. If we claim to be without sin, His word has no place in our lives."

"For if you forgive men when they sin against you, your heavenly Father will also forgive you. But if you do not forgive men their sins, your Father will not forgive your sins."
(MATT. 6:14–15 NIV)

"If we say we have no sin, we are only fooling ourselves and refusing to accept the truth. But if we confess our sins to him, he is faithful and just to forgive us and to cleanse us from every wrong. If we claim we have not sinned, we are calling God a liar and showing that his word has no place in our hearts."
(1 JOHN 1:8–10 NLT)

I want you to know that . . .

My friend felt a lot of guilt and shame for so long, thinking that she must have done something wrong. Once she began to tell other people about what had happened to her, she was able to finally believe that she had done nothing wrong, that she was not to blame. Healing began when she was willing to be open and vulnerable. I love the message of Galatians 6:2, "Share each other's troubles and problems, and in this way obey the law of Christ" (NLT). When my friend put this verse into action, she was set free.

LIVING AND DYING WITHOUT FEAR

In December 2001, I had the amazing privilege of singing at the memorial service for a young soldier who was killed in Afghanistan. A couple days prior to that, our office in Nashville received an e-mail from the parents of Staff Sergeant Brian Cody Prosser's widow. They asked me on behalf of their daughter, Shawna, to come and sing my song, "Wait for Me" at the service. I later found out that my CD *Transform* had been the last gift that he had given to Shawna before leaving for Afghanistan, and "Wait for Me" was "their song."

Not only was it a privilege to sing at his memorial service in Bakersfield, California, but it was also very touching to hear what the different government officials and speakers had to say about Cody's life. One man said something that I will not soon forget: "The courageous do not live forever, but the timid never live at all." Cody's brave death and those words taught me a thing or two about life. If we are living in fear, we are not really living.

Sometimes because of hurts in the past, we fear relationships with the opposite sex. I have a friend whose parents recently divorced. He has had a very hard time allowing anyone special into his life because of fear that she might reject him like his dad had rejected his mom. But our fears keep us in bondage and make us believe Satan's lies instead of God's hopeful plan for our future. My friend desperately needed to know that through God's power it could be a new day, and the decisions of his parents did not have to affect the new generation that he and his wife would one day begin.

Fear has been something I have had to deal with in my own life as well. Even though I have mostly had guy friends and have rarely been romantically involved, I have experienced my own hurts. Coming from a different culture, I didn't know that in America it's pretty standard to say, "I just want to be friends," when really you didn't want to see that person again. I really did want to be friends with some particular guys that liked me, but they took it as rejection, and in turn they rejected me. I had to deal with what has become an expectation of rejection and let go of feeling as if I deserved payback when I honestly showed that I wanted to be friends and nothing more.

For you, maybe the hurt goes a lot deeper and you may have given your heart or even your body to someone, and now you fear that the same thing will happen again. Know that this fear is not of God. If you have given your sin to God, you are completely forgiven, not condemned, and your future is brand-new, with no mistakes.

In the story *Anne of Green Gables*, Anne held on to a grudge that she had against Gilbert. She felt hurt by something he had done when she was twelve years old and held it against him for years. It wasn't until her teacher, Miss Stacey, told her, "Tomorrow is always fresh—with no mistakes in it" that she released the power of holding on to hurts. Hurt holding and future fearing both injure the *now*!

> "There is no room in love for fear. Well-formed love banishes fear. Since fear is crippling, a fearful life—fear of death, fear of judgment—is one not yet fully formed in love."
> (1 JOHN 4:18 THE MESSAGE)

SEND THE BIRD AWAY

Recently I performed at a convention for Christian counselors at the Opryland Hotel in Nashville, Tennessee. My team and I happened to meet a counselor from Australia who is actually related to a distant cousin of mine. (Small world!) In light of this we felt a rather immediate connection with him and fell into a deep conversation about the common problem of worry. He shared a wonderful analogy that has really helped me to let go of worrisome fears.

Our new counselor friend likened worry to a bird. If you let this bird of unhealthy, nonreality-based fears nest or roost in your mind, it can wreak all kinds of havoc. Instead, what we must do with these fears is not let them roost but fly overhead—over top of us. This is a very practical tool to use in deflecting thoughts of past or future rejection and hurt. The answer is to ask God for forgiveness, forgive yourself, and forgive the person who injured you. Memorize Jeremiah 29:11:

> "For I know the plans I have for you," declares the LORD, "plans to prosper you and not to harm you, plans to give you hope and a future. Then you will call upon me and come and pray to me, and I will listen to you. You will seek me and find me when you seek me with all your heart."

If the hurt or fearful thoughts come back, surrender them again to God and let them fly over your head and far away!

> "For God did not give us a spirit of timidity, but a spirit of power, of love, and of self-discipline."
> (2 TIM. 1:7 NIV)

> "Have I not commanded you? Be strong and courageous. Do not be terrified; do not be discouraged, for the LORD your God will be with you wherever you go."
> (JOSH. 1:9 NIV)

Today I wanted to tell you . . .

A BRAND-NEW START

Here's another testimony of a woman who experienced sex before marriage, but was given a second chance:

"I am a mother of three, and I pray daily that my children will be able to remain pure. I was not so fortunate. I became sexually active when I was sixteen years old. By the time I was seventeen, I had been convicted by the Holy Spirit, repented, and been given a second virginity. God displayed further mercy and grace by allowing me to actually marry the one and only person with whom I had been sexually active. However, the emotional and spiritual consequences were horrible. I had no idea it would literally take me years to overcome my disobedience in the area of purity.

"Our marriage suffered in the first several years, even though we had never been with another. I don't think anyone tried to tell me I would suffer so greatly, but I am here to testify that it is definitely not worth anything to disobey God in the area of purity (or any area at all)!"

"Soak me in your laundry and I'll come out clean, scrub me and I'll have a snow-white life. Tune me in to foot-tapping songs, set these once-broken bones to dancing. Don't look too close for blemishes, give me a clean bill of health."
(Ps. 51:7–9 The Message)

If you've already messed up, realize that God will give you a new start . . . if you want it. But you have to desire it. Your physical virginity may be lost, but virginity is more than just physical. It's an attitude, a way of thinking. It's demonstrated in the way you look at yourself and others. It's all about accepting God's forgiveness in your life, then forgiving yourself, believing that you really *can* change bad habits and receive God's healing for past wounds. Just because you made a mistake in the past doesn't mean you have to keep on making the same mistakes. I don't know who said it first, but I like this quote: "You can't change the past, so perfect the future."

HOW DO YOU DO IT?

Former supermodel Kim Alexis offers these five practical steps on her Web site:

1. Make a firm commitment to save yourself for marriage from now on, and believe you can do it.
2. Get away from people, places, things, and situations that weaken your self-control. Sometimes the healthiest thing we can do is avoid people who tempt us.
3. Avoid intense hugging, passionate kissing, and anything else that leads to lustful thoughts and behavior. Anything beyond a brief, simple kiss can quickly become dangerous.
4. Find nonphysical ways to show your love and appreciation.

5. Remember that anyone can start over, including you. When you focus on commitment and self-discipline, you can control your impulses.[1]

> "Now we look inside, and what we see is that anyone united with the Messiah gets a fresh start, is created new. The old life is gone; a new life burgeons! Look at it! All this comes from the God who settled the relationship between us and him, and then called us to settle our relationships with each other. God put the world square with himself through the Messiah, giving the world a fresh start by offering forgiveness of sins."
>
> (2 Cor. 5:17–18 The Message)

Father God, I ask for Your forgiveness of my sin. Help me to forgive myself. You see the deepest parts of my heart. You know my mistakes. You know my regrets. You know my guilt. I want to be able to stand clean before Your presence. I want to live without fear. Thank You for changing my blood-red sins into a blanket of snow-white purity. I accept Your healing.

Thank You, Jesus, for taking my sins to the cross.

In Your merciful name, Amen.

I'm Glad You Asked!

Work had begun on my "Wait for Me" music video. We held auditions for the role of the fictional "guy I was waiting for"—to no avail. As I watched the screen-test audition tapes, I realized we were still a long way off from finding the right young man to play the part. My friend Amy told me she knew a model who had music-video experience and might be willing to give it a go. After a few calls he was on his way from New York to Nashville—and he did a great job! Here's what he wrote to me a few months after filming the video:

> I just want to let you know that first I love the album, and second, I'm doing my part to be an example for Christ. I don't know that I ever told you that I am a Christian. In fact, the biggest reason I got into modeling was to be an example of Jesus in a business that was, and is, so corrupt. It hasn't been easy.

I recently moved to Hollywood to focus on my music and modeling and found a world without God. Wait, I take that back, they do have their gods—coke, X, and heroin, not to mention the drinks. It has been very hard to tolerate, but I do believe that God is using me. I have made my beliefs very clear, and I am respected for it. You should see the faces of the people when I tell them of my abstinence. It's hilarious! It makes me so proud. Anyway, thank you so much for using me in your video. I'm glad to be a part of something that is so profound and good.

CHAPTER *seven*

I'm Glad You Asked!

Q & A ON SEXUAL PURITY

Darling, wait for me . . .

IN HIS POWER

We have received so many letters and e-mails concerning the song "Wait for Me." In fact, we have received more responses about this song than anything else I have ever recorded. It has definitely struck a nerve in the hearts of listeners all around the world. I would like to conclude the book by answering some of the most-asked questions we have received, in hopes that the practical advice offered will give you some spiritual ammo in this quest to recapture the dream and stand firm in sexual purity.

Q: HOW CAN I RESIST THE URGE TO HAVE SEX OUTSIDE OF MARRIAGE, ESPECIALLY IF I'VE ALREADY HAD SEX BEFORE?

A: The only way that we can resist the desire to sin is by relying on God's strength. I would encourage you to turn to God and pray for His power to stand strong. I recently spoke with a friend of mine who had experienced sex before she was married and this is some of the advice she had to pass on:

> "I see now that what I thought was 'showing him love' was really the opposite of that; it was selfishness, it was lust, and it was not of God. Putting yourself in situations in which things *can* happen is a really bad idea—because things *will* happen. Jesus said, 'The spirit is willing, but the flesh is weak.' That's why the Bible says to 'flee temptation'—you don't run to it.
>
> "I understand now that Satan was feeding me a lie that I was unworthy and unforgivable, and I believed it. That lie helped encourage me to continue in that lifestyle of having sex before I was married. Whenever I would try to

stop us sleeping together, I always tried in my own power, not in God's power, and it never lasted."

The only way to live a life of purity is through God's power!

> "Now glory be to God. By his mighty power at work within us, he is able to accomplish infinitely more-than we would ever dare to ask or hope."
> (EPH. 3:20 NLT)

Q: Can you share some practical ways to stay pure in mind and heart, and not just in body?

A: This question hits on a very important point. Unless there is a commitment to purity of the mind and heart, then there is not much hope for purity of the body. A daily devotional time with God is essential for heart, mind, and body purity. Ephesians 5:26 tells us that we are made clean by the washing of the Word. When we spend time with God, the things of this world fade into the background. As I mentioned earlier in the book, watching what you feed your mind is incredibly important. If you put junk in, junk stays, and junk will come out in your life. Build good, solid friendships with people who will encourage you in heart, mind, and body purity. Any of Elisabeth Eliot's books would be an encouragement to you in this area as well.

Q: How are you supposed to be "just friends" with a guy?

A: I believe that it is possible to be "just friends" with members of the opposite sex. For this friendship to take place, I think you have to be willing to be up front about the fact that you do not want romance to "cloud" the relationship (although some of the best marriages come from strong friendships!). It is much more difficult if you have been romantically interested in each other. Often one of the people involved in the friendship will "hang on," hoping for something more. For a real friendship to flourish in that situation, it takes wisdom, prayer, patience, and a commitment to honesty.

If you know that someone is attracted to you, but you only desire a friendship, I think it is important that you let the other person know. Try not to be overly friendly. In that way you are helping to "guard their heart" and you're also avoiding needless, messy problems. While we're single, friendships with members of the opposite sex are extremely valuable.

Q: How far is too far in sexual sin? Is there a definite way to tell?

A: That is a very good question. A popular Christian magazine for teens, *Campus Life*, interviewed me, and they said that this question is asked more than perhaps any other.

Here are several practical guidelines when it comes to setting physical boundaries. The first rule is to stay away from touching any part of the body that is covered by a two-piece bathing suit. Pretty self-explanatory. The second rule is this: don't let anything belonging to your body enter anything belonging to someone else's body. That should about cover it: from sexual intercourse to oral sex, to stimulating your partner's sex organs. If you think about it, even French kissing is an oral form of intercourse. There are some differences of opinion here, but here's the important question to ask yourself: will participating in this activity lead me to do other things that definitely go beyond my desire for sexual purity? Be honest with yourself, be honest with your boyfriend or girlfriend, and be honest with God.

It is also a bad idea to begin to take off any part of clothing. And, girls, even if you are still both wearing your clothes, I think for a guy to lie on top of you is simply inviting trouble. As I said earlier, if you would have a hard time explaining to your future spouse what you did with someone else, then it's probably not a good idea. Most important, if you know you'd have a hard time defending your actions before God on Judgment Day, then you definitely shouldn't be "going there."

> "But the LORD is faithful, and he will strengthen and protect
> you from the evil one."
> (2 THESS. 3:3 NIV)

Q: What if God chooses for me to be single my whole life? Would I become bitter and angry at God because of this?

A: In my mind, it would be better to be single than to marry the wrong person, and if God has not brought that right person, you're crazy to just marry out of loneliness or fear that you're going to be left behind.

As for the "bitter and angry" part, that is our choice. If we truly accept that God has a plan for us and if we wholly trust Him with our lives, how can we be angry at God, thinking we know better than He what our lives should look like? I have come to the conclusion that I know God has not called me to spend all my time in search of a husband. I do believe that God has a plan for me (Jer. 29:11), that He will supply all my needs according to His glorious riches (Phil. 4:19), and that He wants me to trust Him completely (Prov. 3:4–6).

> "Trust in the LORD and do good; dwell in the land and enjoy safe pasture. Delight yourself in the LORD and he will give you the desires of your heart. Commit your way to the LORD; trust in him and he will do this: He will make your righteousness shine like the dawn, the justice of your cause like the noonday sun. Be still before the LORD and wait patiently for him; do not fret when men succeed in their ways, when they carry out wicked schemes."
>
> (Ps. 37:3–7 NIV)

Q: How do I find someone who is well-grounded in her faith? Is there anything I should be doing on my part besides praying?

A: Praying is the main thing you and I can be doing for our future spouses and our future marriages right now. I met a guy at an "Acquire the Fire" youth convention who asked, "Should I just wait for God to drop a girl in my lap, or should I be acting in some proactive way while I am waiting?"

I don't believe that God would have us to be club hopping or even singles-group jumping to find the man or woman of our dreams. Our responsibility as a godly single person is to be open to relationships with the opposite sex, to be willing to be vulnerable, and not closed off. Problems often begin when people are so concerned with having their walls up that they're not willing to create friendships with the opposite sex.

I believe that our part is to seek Him first and to simply be open. God wants us to be willing to be vulnerable, and to get to know people, but not to fear. Ultimately, by my trying to force God's hand or "help Him out" by orchestrating this, that, or the other, I will only wind up more frustrated, lonely, and worried about being alone.

Every now and then when I start to get concerned about how long God is going to take in this "husband bringing" process, it's almost as if God encourages me with a little forward thought. An image comes to mind of me, one day in the future, happily settled with my husband, wondering why I ever worried that God would not provide!

> "We humans keep brainstorming options and plans, but God's *purpose prevails*."
>
> (Prov. 19:21 The Message, emphasis mine)

Q: I want to write a poem to my future husband. Can you help me?

A: I may not have written a poem to my future husband, but I have definitely written love letters to him! I have also written a certain love song called "Wait for Me" (and I suppose poems come from a similar family). In my love letters I address my future husband familiarly, as if I've known him for a long time (which, by the time he reads them, will be true!). I often write my letters when I am feeling particularly lonely for him, so I express my thoughts to that end.

I've shared different thoughts and feelings relevant to my life at that particular time, so that he will be able to "see into" snippets of my life at different stages. I have even expressed a little about what I think he might be like as a person, which will be funny one day, depending on how far or close to the mark I was! I have also shared some of my dreams and things that I would like to do together in our future. There are some ideas for you!

Q: If you don't have sex with someone before you marry, how do you know that you're sexually compatible?

A: One of the problems I have with this question is that it makes it sound as though you're buying a horse. You shouldn't choose a life partner based on his or her sexual performance. It's not the main issue here. God created us to be able to enjoy sex for pleasure in the context of a marriage relationship. (That's what the Old Testament book Song of Songs is all about.) The other purpose is to be able to have children, to allow future generations to exist. My dad has said that knowing each other's sexual needs in marriage doesn't happen overnight and needs to be worked at. I think the old adage of "practice makes perfect" seems pretty applicable. Living together before marriage is morally wrong and is not in God's plan for our lives.

To me the more obvious need in relationships is for patience and understanding—to learn what makes your spouse feel most loved. It is all about serving one another in love. I truly feel that as humans we cannot give ourselves emotionally and physically in full to someone in sex unless there is complete trust in that person. How are you going to fully trust someone who can't commit to life with you in marriage?

> "The marriage bed must be a place of mutuality—the husband seeking to satisfy his wife, the wife seeking to satisfy her husband. Marriage is not a place to 'stand up for your

rights.' Marriage is a decision to serve the other, whether in
bed or out."

(1 Cor. 7:3–4 The Message)

Q: How do you talk about God's idea of sexual purity to unsaved friends without sounding as though you think you are better than them?

A: A purity ring or a purity necklace is always a good "in" to talk about sexual purity. If someone asks you a question about it, just as if someone asks you about your faith, it is always a very natural door of opportunity to share about God's way. Then I believe the best way to talk about your decision to wait and how you came to that decision (from your commitment to Jesus) is to be very honest and real. Talk about your experiences in life with God and about what brought you to make the decision to wait. People are much less offended and much less likely to think you're "stuffy" and "religious" if they see that you're being honest with them.

If your friends who have asked about sexual abstinence believe what you share with them, then maybe in the future you will have an opportunity to share about God's "second chance." Really pray for God's timing on this. It may be that God could lead you to talk to your friends about His forgiveness. Pray and be led by Him.

"Live wisely among those who are not Christians, and make
the most of every opportunity. Let your conversation be

gracious and effective so that you will have the right answer for everyone."

(Col. 4:5-6 NLT)

Q: I know that God is to be my true focus while I'm single, but I struggle with making Him that, and not being distracted by my desire for love. How can I make God my main focus?

A: Did you know that you can experience the most powerful, beautiful romance with God Himself? You can. Over the last few years God has given me a growing awareness that unless my love for Him is first, I am incapable of enjoying human love completely. A true foundational love for God must be central in my own life; otherwise everything else is thrown off balance. One of the things that has helped me a lot in this quest for a deeper, abiding first-love relationship with God is the time I spend walking with Him.

Sometimes I'll go on a moonlit walk, just God and me (and maybe the dogs traipsing behind), and I'll just pour out my heart to Him. Often I will have a sense that God is wrapping His arms around me, holding me, comforting me, drawing me close. It is the most amazing feeling of joy ever, and I don't know how a human love could possibly compare to the deep-seated peace that *His* love brings. Draw deeper into romance with God—He is the greatest lover of all!

"Commit to the LORD whatever you do, and your plans will succeed."

(PROV. 16:3 NIV)

In this book we have discovered that we need to dream again, we need to push the reset button in the field of romance. My hope for you is that you have done just that. We have also come to understand the incredibly important role the mind plays in protecting purity. We have read about the horrific consequences of going against God's plan for sex, and we have rediscovered the beauty and joy of purity in romance.

I am enjoying this season of singleness, and in this book I have shared ways you can enjoy this time as well. I dream about getting married one day and am praying that God will prepare me for that time. I hope and pray that God has used these pages to draw you closer to Him and to solidify your commitment to purity in relationships. I pray also that God's truth has helped bring healing from the hurt of shattered dreams and painful mistakes and restored belief in God's beautiful plan for your life.

May God bless and keep you as, in purity, you journey on.

"The LORD your God is with you, he is mighty to save. He will take great delight in you, he will quiet you with his love, he will rejoice over you with singing."

(ZEPH. 3:17 NIV)

Lord Jesus, I come to You knowing that You have the answers for my every need. You know my thoughts. You know my desires for the future. I want to please You with my mind, my heart, my body—my all. Holy Spirit, fill me to over-flowing. I need You. I need Your strength to walk in holiness. Lord, I give my life afresh to You, to glorify You. I commit from this day on to live a life dedicated to sexual purity. Help me to flee temptation but run to You. I will wait because I honor You.

In Your precious name, Amen.

Wait for Me
Study Guide

CHAPTER ONE

I believe that God has placed "The Dream" inside every person, unless He has specifically called you to singleness. We each have a desire for intimacy, for someone to know us fully and love us completely. We long to be able to share our hearts and still find acceptance.

What dreams do you have about your future spouse? How do you imagine meeting him or her? What do you think that person will be like?

What about marriage do you most look forward to?

Read Psalm 139. It is one of my favorite passages in the Bible. It amazes me to think that God knows everything about me, that He knows everything I do, and that He was dreaming and planning for me before I was even born. Did you ever think about why God made you exactly the way you are? Why do you love piano or comedies or books? Why are you shy or talkative or funny? Did you ever think that God might have made you that way for a reason—that who you are and the way you are is part of the dreams He has for your life?

What do you think God enjoys about you?

QUIZ:
ARE YOU A DREAMER?

How much do you dream about the future? Are you so caught up in your own dreams that it's hard to listen to God's ideas? Or are you so down-to-earth and realistic that it's hard for you to imagine the adventures God has for you?

1. What do you want to be when you grow up?
   a. Rich, famous, successful, godly, and happy
   b. The best at something I love
   c. Just happy
   d. Do I have to grow up?

2. What do you most look forward to right now?
   a. Growing up, getting married, having a job and a family I love
   b. Graduating from college and entering "the real world"
   c. Finishing my next test
   d. The weekend!

3. How much time do you spend daydreaming?
   a. I'm very focused on the here and now.
   b. I daydream right before I fall asleep at night.
   c. My friends and I are always talking about our dreams and plans.
   d. What did you say? I wasn't paying attention.

4. What aspect of your future spouse do you think about the most?
   a. The way he (or she) will look
   b. The way he (or she) will treat me
   c. The way I'll treat him (or her)
   d. I've never thought about it.

5. How much of your wedding do you have planned?
   a. I've never given it a second thought.
   b. I noticed a couple of good ideas at my cousin's wedding.
   c. I've figured out just about everything, except the groom (or bride)!
   d. I've planned the whole thing, and I even made a mix of romantic tunes for the wedding night.

Sometimes people prevent their dreams from being realized by holding on to them too tightly. But the more we cling to them, the more we destroy them. The dreams that God meant to be beautiful can easily become twisted and broken by our past, our culture, and our inability to let go.

The world tells us that if we believe in our dreams then we have to make them happen. But God promises that He will fulfill the dreams He has for us—in His perfect way and in His perfect timing. Only then will they become dreams that are worth living.

Look up the word **surrender** in your dictionary and write its meaning here.

If you were to surrender your dreams completely to God, what would the outcome be?

Surrender is a lot like death. The loss hurts, and it's hard. It requires giving up everything you dreamed about for the future. But the beauty of surrender is that God promises a resurrection— and the revival of the dream is much more beautiful than anything you could imagine on your own. It's not until we are willing to give up our dreams that God is able to reset and restart our dreams, transforming them beyond all hope.

In what ways have your past experiences influenced your thinking about God's plans for you?

Do you think the culture has shaped your way of dreaming? If so, why?

CHAPTER TWO

If the eyes are "windows to the soul," then we should be very careful what we allow to gain entry into our minds through them.

When you're lying in bed just about to fall asleep, what do you usually think about?

What's the first thing you think about when you wake up in the morning?

What we read, listen to, and experience—the things we do—become the things we think. And the Bible tells us that what we think ultimately becomes what we are. Wow! That's frightening—

the things you put into your mind will ultimately become what you are. Just like the saying, "You are what you eat," you could almost say that, in the long run, "You are what you see and hear."

What are three things that you like to do in your free time?

What were the last three movies you saw? The last two books you read? The last CD you bought? How does their content affect you?

Look again at your list of recent activities, and ask yourself: do these things represent the kind of person I want to be?

God, I confess the negative things I have put into my mind by . . .

From now on, my standards for what I put into my mind will be . . .

It's compromise in little areas that often leads to bad decisions later. It's strength and courage shown in the "small" tests of life that make the "big" decisions easy.

How many of your friends outside of church know that you're a Christian?

How do people know what you believe?

We can be pure without being offensive. If we set an example in a way that is appropriate and encouraging, not only will it affect our lives positively, it can influence and inspire everyone around us.

Have you ever given in on one of your standards because of outside pressure? Explain what happened.

Have you ever offended someone who wasn't a believer because you held a personal conviction in a way that was confrontational and judgmental? Think about it.

Because I want to avoid even a hint of evil in any aspect of my life, I commit myself to the following standards:

Regarding friendships with those of the opposite sex:

Regarding dating relationships:

Regarding food, drink, clothes, and entertainment:

Regarding places I go:

CHAPTER THREE

Those who are trying to please God shouldn't be asking how close to the edge they can go before crossing the line. Christians should be more concerned with how close they can get to God.

How good are you at accomplishing the goals you set for yourself?

What about keeping the limits you set for yourself?

It's probably the most common question asked about the issue of physical intimacy: How far is too far? How much can you do with your date before you're officially sinning? Many teens wonder exactly at what point do you cross the line?

On the issue of levels of physical intimacy before marriage, the Bible is strangely silent. Scripture is very clear that sex outside of marriage is not God's plan for us, but it says nothing about kissing, hugging, "making out," or all the different levels of intimacy that lead up to the act of sex. The specifics of "how far is too far" are left entirely up to us to discern.

This is a problem because . . .

What reasons can you think of for having some level of physical affection in a dating relationship?

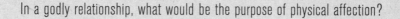

In a godly relationship, what would be the purpose of physical affection?

Ask yourself: Is the level of affection in your relationship helping you to experience God's love, or is it encouraging lust? To flesh out these hard answers, continue to break it down by asking: Where are you trying to go with this relationship, and especially with the physical part of it? Where will each action lead you, and what are the consequences? This process will help you decide where to set limits regarding sexual intimacy.

How else can you discern for yourself how far is too far, and set healthy limits?

What level of physical intimacy in a dating relationship do you believe would be most honoring to God?

Right now, I make a commitment to not go beyond the following limitations of physical intimacy until I am married:

What do you think are the greatest dangers of sex outside of marriage?

For you, what would be the worst possible consequence of having sex?

The most common answers to that question are probably pregnancy and STDs. Both of those are terrible and difficult consequences, often with lifelong physical effects. It is important that we realize the powerful emotional and spiritual consequences that sex has on our lives. Just one sexual act can have consequences that affect us, our friends, our families, our future spouses, and our children for years to come.

My reasons for waiting:

- the dangers of sex:

- my love for my future spouse:

- the consequences in my family:

- the consequences to my Christian witness:

- others:

It may be that you have already experienced the terrible consequences of sex outside of marriage. Or maybe you haven't actually had sex, but you've gone further physically than you believe God wanted you to. The beauty of our God is that He always stands ready and willing to forgive us. Take a few minutes to reflect on God's forgiveness.

Lord, I know that You have forgiven me because . . .
(Write out passages of Scripture that promise His forgiveness. If you can't find any, ask a parent, youth pastor, or Bible study leader to help you.)

God, Your forgiveness makes me feel . . .

I thank You because . . .

CHAPTER FOUR

Don't pine about the house waiting for your prince or princess to come along! God made this world, this life, for us to enjoy, and subsequently praise Him for.

Describe your personality in three words.

What are your best character traits?

What are your worst faults?

While it's easy to focus on what you want in a relationship, it's much harder to focus on who you need to be in order to be the right person for such a relationship. If you want to marry a great, godly person, the first step is to for you to become a great, godly person.

When was the last time you went out of your way to serve someone else?

Who was the last person you prayed for?

Which do you spend more time doing—asking God for things or thanking Him for what He's given you?

QUIZ:
ARE YOU READY FOR TRUE LOVE?

Before you can find "the one," you need to be "the one."
How close are you? If God were to bring the perfect future
spouse into your life right now, would they even be
attracted to you? Are you the kind of person who would
attract a godly man or woman? Take this quiz to find out!

1. What kinds of things do you usually pray for?
   a. A romantic relationship is the number one thing on
      your list!
   b. God is like Santa—you spend all your prayer time
      telling Him your list.
   c. You mostly thank Him for things He's done for you.
   d. You don't pray much.

2. How often do you read the Bible?
   a. Once a week, in church
   b. Twice a week, in church and at youth group
   c. Every once in a while on your own
   d. You don't have a Bible.

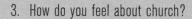

3. How do you feel about church?
   a. You go only when your parents make you.
   b. You enjoy hanging out with your church friends.
   c. You're there every time they open the doors—when your parents want to punish you, they ground you from youth group.

Whether God has called us to be married or single, it really comes down to the same thing—making Him our first love, focusing our gaze on Him.

What is the best part about not being in a romantic relationship?

What is the worst part?

What if God intends for you to remain single for your entire life? What are some possible ways that you could use the freedom of being single to serve Him more effectively?

What is something you do for yourself, God, or others that you promise not to give up when you get married?

Lord, thank You for the gift of singleness that You have given me for this stage of my life. I am grateful for it because . . .

I will use it to serve You by . . .

I will seek to make You my first love by . . .

CHAPTER FIVE

Your marriage will never be a happy one as long as you are just looking out for yourself. Over and over I have heard couples, including my own parents, say that their marriage only became great when they learned to give, love, and serve more than they sought to receive. This is a principle we can be practicing now because it is a life principle, not just one that applies to marriage. Whenever we choose to serve ourselves, selfishness—not to mention unhappiness—grows. But when we give our lives up completely to God, to love and serve Him and then others, joy reigns in our hearts.

What do you hope to gain from being married? What do you hope to give to your marriage?

What does unconditional love mean to you?

When we're in love, the reaction is the same. We want to serve the person we love; it becomes incredibly easy to serve, and it's impossible to imagine that the desire to encourage and serve him could ever diminish. Time floats by in a blur, and we barely even notice. All we want is to be around him, and we're willing to make any sacrifice to make him happy. It would be nice if that state of mind really could last forever. But it doesn't.

Unfortunately, the passion to serve another that is so natural under the influence of early romance quickly becomes just as challenging and difficult as serving any of the ordinary people in our lives. That is why the best way we can prepare to serve our spouses for the rest of their lives is by serving the people around us now.

How can you serve the people closest to you? Your family and closest friends? List three people and three specific ways you can serve each one.

What types of service are really hard for you? How can you make opportunities to do those kinds of service?

QUIZ:
ARE YOU READY FOR TRUE LOVE?

How much have you already developed the discipline of service? Are you a selfish brat or a humble servant? Answer these questions to find out!

1. When you see someone drop all their books in the middle of a busy hallway, you:
   a. Laugh at them.
   b. Stop and help as long as you're not already running late.
   c. Drop whatever you're doing to help them pick up the books.
   d. Help them pick up the books and listen for an opportunity to talk with them about your faith while you're doing it.

2. When your friends want to go do something fun, you:
    a. Only go if they'll agree to an activity that you pick.
    b. Usually let someone else choose what you're doing; you just enjoy spending time with them.
    c. Always pick everyone up, because you're the only one with a car.
    d. Are always too busy to go.

3. When it comes to housework, you:
    a. Can't tell a dust rag from a mop.
    b. Help your mom out occasionally on the weekends.
    c. Regularly ask your parents if there are ways that you can help out.
    d. Do pretty much everything; you're in charge of all the housework around here!
    e. Do a lot of it but also help teach your younger brothers and sisters how to sort laundry or mow the lawn.

Make a list of some practical ideas for ways to practice service in your life right now.

Most people have some idea of the personality traits, physical characteristics, and character qualities they're looking for in the person they want to marry. I think it's good to keep a clear idea of what you want and what God wants for you, but also to stay open to surprises that God might choose to bring into your life. However, there are some things we should never compromise on in relationships. When you're considering spending the rest of your life joined with another person, there are certain character traits that you should insist that he or she have before you even consider a relationship with someone.

What are the three most important traits you want your future spouse to have?

Lord, I pray for the person You have chosen for me to someday marry. Although I don't know him (or her), I know that You know everything about him (or her). I pray that You would keep him (or her) safe from physical, emotional, and spiritual dangers. Please begin now to prepare him (or her) for marriage by . . .

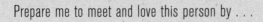

Prepare me to meet and love this person by . . .

Grow this person to be like You, especially in Your . . .

CHAPTER SIX

Forgiveness is not an option. If we belong to Christ, then God has forgiven us; therefore we have no right to not forgive others, or ourselves.

What is the worst thing you've ever been forgiven for?

What is the hardest thing you've ever had to forgive?

Even the worst betrayal a human could ever experience, such as the betrayal of a wife to her husband, doesn't compare with what we as God's creation have done to Him when we turn away from Him. And yet God has already forgiven us, and He gladly takes us back. When we consider the depth of God's forgiveness toward us, it becomes a little easier to forgive.

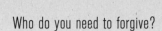

Who do you need to forgive?

How can you accept the power of God's forgiveness for that person?

The means by which we can forgive others is the same means by which God forgives us—by accepting Christ's punishment as payment for that sin against us, thus allowing the person who deserves that punishment, who did that wrong, to go free, forgiven.

I have been wronged and hurt by others by . . .

Jesus, I know that You paid for those sins by Your death on the cross. I accept Your payment for those sins in place of the people who deserve them. From now on, help me to demonstrate Your love and forgiveness to these people by . . .

Fear is one of the greatest obstacles to our fulfilling God's purpose in our lives. Especially when it comes to relationships, fear is often one of the main reasons why things don't go as they should. If we are living in fear, we are not really living.

What are your biggest fears about relationships?

What situations tend to bring out your fears?

What decisions have you made recently that were based in fear?

Fear doesn't have to control your life or your decisions. In fact, God commands us not to be dominated by fear.

> "Remember that I commanded you to be strong and brave.
> Don't be afraid, because the LORD your God will be with you
> everywhere you go."
> (JOSH. 1:9 NCV)

How can you overcome fear? Use this list as a starting point, and prayerfully add your own thoughts about facing your fears:

Do things you're afraid of.
Share your fears with friends and ask them to pray for you.
Confess your fears to God.

Write down and then memorize Scripture passages about God's protection, trustworthiness, and control, and remember them when you're afraid.

Lord, I know that You don't want for my life to be controlled by fear. I have been afraid of . . .

I know that You have control over my life, and I trust that You . . .

ABOUT THE AUTHOR

A multiple Dove Award winner as well as a winner of America's most prestigious musical award—the Grammy®—Rebecca St. James has been a major defining female voice in contemporary Christian music since the late 90s. Her groundbreaking album *Pray* most recently achieved RIAA gold record status—following in the footsteps of the previously gold-certified album *God*. In January 2008 she was named "Favorite Female Artist" in the *CCM Magazine* Readers' Choice Awards for the seventh consecutive year. Rebecca also repeated with the "Best Female Artist of 2007" in the Christianitytoday.com Readers' Choice Awards—her fifth consecutive year to be given this honor. *CRW Magazine* has named Rebecca to its list of "50 Most Influential People in Contemporary Music," and her book *Wait for Me* was a #1 Christian Booksellers Association Young Adult bestseller and has sold more than 100,000 copies.

If you've never committed your life to Jesus, or if you need to "get serious" about Him, please pray this prayer . . .

Dear Jesus . . . Thank you so much for loving me even when I don't deserve You at all. Lord, come into my life, change me, break me, make me new, make me whole . . . forgive me. Purify my heart. Jesus I believe You died on the cross and rose again three days later. You are my savior and one day I will live with You forever. But meanwhile, help me to stand for You. To shine for You, to make a difference and let Your truth be known. Use me Lord, Holy Spirit fill me to overflowing. I love You so much! In Jesus' Name, Amen.

NOTES

CHAPTER 1

1. Throughout book: "Wait for Me" by Rebecca St. James, from the *Transform* record. © 2000 Up in the Mix Music (BMI) and Bibbitsong Music (admin. by ICG).
2. "When the Dream Never Dies," from the *Child of the Promise* soundtrack (Sparrow Records), © 2000 Mandipher Music and Just Enough Light Music. All rights reserved. Used by permission.

CHAPTER 2

1. Words and music by John Thompson and Randy Scruggs/© 1982 Whole Armor Music and Full Armor Music/Administered by The Kruger Organization, Inc. International copyright secured./All rights reserved. Used by permission.

CHAPTER 3

1. Statistics taken from the U.S. Department of Health and Human Services and the Centers for Disease Control and Prevention, September 1998.
2. "Scientific Evidence on Condom Effectiveness for Sexually Transmitted Disease Prevention," June 2000.
3. Statistics taken from The Centers for Disease Control and Prevention, September 1998.
4. The Alan Guttmacher Institute, *U.S. Teenage Pregnancy Statistics*, 1997.
5. "Unintended Pregnancy in the United States," *Family Planning Perspectives*, 1998.

CHAPTER 5

1. "I Will Stand By You" by Rebecca St. James.
2. Sheldon Vanauken, *A Severe Mercy* (New York: Bantam Books, 1977), 29.

CHAPTER 6

1. www.lovematters.com/startover.htm

187